JUMPSTART LOGIC PRO X 10.5

Jumpstart Logic Pro X 10.5

CREATE PROFESSIONAL MUSIC WITH APPLE'S FLAGSHIP DIGITAL AUDIO WORKSTATION APP

Jay Asher

BIRMINGHAM—MUMBAI

Jumpstart Logic Pro X 10.5

Jay Asher

Commissioning Editor: Pavan Ramchandani
Acquisition Editor: Apurv Desai
Senior Editor: Sofi Rogers
Content Development Editor: Keagan Carneiro
Technical Editor: Shubham Sharma
Copy Editor: Safis Editing
Project Coordinator: Kinjal Bari
Proofreader: Safis Editing
Indexer: Priyanka Dhadke
Production Designer: Jyoti Chauhan
Technical Production Manager: Joseph Runnacles

First published: October 2020

Production reference: 1301020

Published by Packt Publishing Ltd.
Livery Place
35 Livery Street
Birmingham
B3 2PB, UK.

ISBN 978-1-80056-277-6

WWW.PACKT.COM

To Dr. Gerhard Lengeling, Chris Adam, and all the other members of the Logic development team, past and present, who in 1990, started me on the unlikely journey to become a guy that writes books on music technology.

– Jay Asher

Packt>

Subscribe to our online digital library for full access to over 7,000 books and videos, as well as industry leading tools to help you plan your personal development and advance your career. For more information, please visit our website.

WHY SUBSCRIBE?

- ▶ Spend less time learning and more time coding with practical eBooks and Videos from over 4,000 industry professionals
- ▶ Learn better with Skill Plans built especially for you
- ▶ Get a free eBook or video every month
- ▶ Fully searchable for easy access to vital information
- ▶ Copy and paste, print, and bookmark content

Did you know that Packt offers eBook versions of every book published, with PDF and ePub files available? You can upgrade to the eBook version at www.Packt.com and as a print book customer, you are entitled to a discount on the eBook copy. Get in touch with us at customercare@packtpub.com for more details.

At www.packt.com, you can also read a collection of free technical articles, sign up for a range of free newsletters, and receive exclusive discounts and offers on Packt books and eBooks.

CONTRIBUTORS

ABOUT THE AUTHOR

Jay Asher is an Apple Certified Trainer for Logic Pro X, and the author of *Going Pro with Logic Pro 9* and *Scoring with Logic Pro*. He has been a private consultant for many famous rock stars and film/TV composers. A composer and songwriter himself, Jay Asher scored the TV series *Zorro* and has written songs that have been recorded by Julio Iglesias, Whitney Houston, and Donna Summer, among others. He began learning Logic for his own musical endeavors, but along the way, something funny happened: he became a Logic Pro guru! Find out more at his website www.jayasher.com.

I want to thank all the people who have been so supportive of me over the years especially my wife, Rosemary, my daughter Emily, and my parents.

ABOUT THE REVIEWER

Eli Krantzberg's greatest loves, beside his wife Mariam, are drumming, his vibraphone, and jazz. The leader of a commercial band for three decades, Eli has been demystifying and simplifying music software since 2008. His tutorials, for Logic as well as various other DAWs and plugins, can be found at Groove3, and Logic Pro Expert. During the COVID-19 pandemic, Eli has perfected his garden-watering techniques and is especially proud of his hanging baskets.

TABLE OF CONTENTS

Contributors   vii

PREFACE

1 BEGINNING WITH LOGIC PRO X 10.5

Important information for beginning with Logic Pro X   **23**

What are Audio and MIDI?   **24**

Selecting essential hardware for Logic Pro X 10.5   **24**

An audio interface   24

A MIDI controller   26

Monitor speakers   26

Monitor headphones   27

Preferences versus Project Settings   **27**

Opening Logic Pro X for the very first time!   27

Changing Logic Pro X's default opening behavior   29

Summary   **30**

2 GETTING TO KNOW THE LOGIC PRO X INTERFACE

Logic Pro X windows, menus, and terminology   **31**

The Main Window   31

Tracks versus Channel Strips   33

The Logic Pro X Library   **34**

The Toolbar   36

Customizing the Control bar and Toolbar   36

Logic Pro X's included content   39

Exploring the Browser   **40**

The Project Browser   41

The Media Browser   42

The All Files Browser   43

Apple Loops and the Loop Browser   **44**

Saving your project   47

The Left-click and Command-click tools 48

Snap 49

Changing the key and transposing regions 50

Summary **51**

3 RECORDING AUDIO

The Project Templates **54**

Setting Preferences **56**

Audio Preferences 56

Recording Preferences 58

Display Preferences 59

Project Settings **60**

Setting levels 60

Recording with a Cycle **63**

Cycle recording with Take Folders 63

Quick Swipe Comping 65

Project Alternatives 66

Region Gain 66

Other Cycle audio recording options 66

Recording without a Cycle **67**

Tape recorder style punching in/out **68**

Recording without a click with Smart Tempo **69**

Saving a template **70**

Summary **70**

4 EDITING AUDIO

Soloing and muting tracks and regions **71**

Mute/solo buttons on the Track Header 72

Mute/solo buttons on the channel strip in the Mixer 74

Region solo button in the Control Bar 74

Renaming and colorizing tracks and regions **75**

Zooming in and out on regions **77**

Copying and repeating regions **78**

Copying by holding Option + dragging 78

Copying parts of regions with the Marquee tool 79

Editing with Shuffle Mode 80

Repeat Regions 81

Looping regions 82

Working with an imported audio file in the Audio Track Editor **83**

Audio Track Editor 84

Audio File Editor 85

Summary **86**

5 RECORDING MIDI

Logic Pro X's Software Instruments 87

Logic Pro X's built-in help   88

GarageBand versus Logic Pro
instruments   88

**Viewing a MIDI region in the Logic
Pro MIDI editors   90**

MIDI continuous controllers   92

Recording MIDI with Merge   92

Let's get started!   92

Advanced Quantize parameters   94

Setting a default quantization
setting   95

**Other techniques for recording
MIDI   95**

Recording MIDI with Replace   95

Recording MIDI with Cycle and

Merge   96

Recording MIDI with Cycle and
Create Tracks   96

Recording MIDI with Cycle and
Create Track Alternatives   97

Recording MIDI with Cycle and
Take Folders   98

Recording MIDI with CCs   98

The Arpeggiator MIDI FX plugin   99

Creating patches   101

Creating a layered patch with
Summing Stacks   101

Creating a split layered patch
with Summing Stacks   102

Groove Tracks   104

Summary   105

6 STEP ENTERING AND EDITING MIDI

**Step entering in the Piano Roll
Editor   107**

The Velocity slider   110

The Velocity Tool   111

Scale Quantize   112

Time Quantize   113

Using the Step Input Keyboard   114

MIDI Transform   116

Time Handles   118

**Entering MIDI controller steps in
the Piano Roll Editor   118**

Creating a crescendo by MIDI
velocity   119

Creating vibrato with modulation 119

A brief look at the Step Editor   121

Summary   121

7 LOGIC PRO X'S DRUMMER

Getting familiar with Drummer and the Library	**123**	Adding a percussionist	132
Arrangement Global Track	**127**	**Drum Machine Designer**	**133**
Converting a Drummer region into a MIDI region	129	Drum Machine Designer editor	135
		Drum Synth	**136**
Customizing a Drum Kit Designer drum kit	**130**	**Drummer Loops**	**136**
		Summary	**138**
Producer Kits	131		

8 LOGIC PRO X'S STEP SEQUENCER

Getting familiar with the Step Sequencer	**139**	The Step Sequencer Local Inspector	144
Pattern Regions	141	**The Pattern Browser**	**145**
Creating Steps in the Pattern Region	143	**Pattern Loops**	**147**
Editing rows and sounds	144	**Summary**	**148**

9 WORKING WITH SAMPLER, QUICK SAMPLER, AND AUTO SAMPLER

Loading instruments into Sampler	**151**	Recording into Quick Sampler	157
Working with Quick Sampler	**151**	Exporting drum slices to create a Drum Machine Designer track	158
Loading Apple Loops to Quick Sampler	152	**Getting familiar with Auto Sampler**	**158**
Importing existing audio files into Quick Sampler	157	**Summary**	**160**

10 WORKING WITH LIVE LOOPS

Understanding Cells and Scenes with a Starter grid	**161**	**Creating scenes from cells**	**166**
Editing cells	**165**	**Recording into cells**	**168**

Recording a performance to the Tracks area 168

Logic Remote 169

Novation Launchpad and Launchkey MIDI controllers 170

Remix FX 170

Overview 170

Capturing Remix FX with Automation 172

Summary 173

11 WORKING WITH AUDIO FILES, TEMPO, AND PITCH

Adjusting a project's tempo with an imported audio file using Smart Tempo 175

Fixing the timing of audio files with Flex Time 177

Fixing the pitch of a vocal with Flex Pitch 178

Varispeed 181

Summary 182

12 GETTING THE ARRANGEMENT RIGHT

What really matters in your arrangement? 183

Know your genre 184

Know your strengths and weaknesses 184

Creating a Project Alternative 184

Adding a section to your arrangement 186

Insert Silence at Locators 186

Repeat Section Between Locators 190

Deleting a section of your arrangement 191

Cut Section Between Locators 192

Consolidating regions and converting MIDI to audio files 192

Bounce Track In Place 195

Bounce Regions In Place 197

Bounce and Replace All Tracks 197

Export Tracks and Regions 198

Freeze tracks 201

Summary 202

13 ORGANIZING FOR THE MIX

Getting familiar with Folder Stacks 204

Creating Folder Stacks 204

Folder Stacks and the Mixer 207

Mixer views 208

Tracks view 208

Single view 209

All view 209

The Environment – a brief overview 210

Creating customized Screensets 211

Creating a locked custom Screenset 211

Duplicating a custom Screenset to create another 214

Creating Markers 215

Creating markers in the Marker track 215

Navigating your project with Marker key commands 217

Creating a Cycle from a Marker 219

Editing Markers in the Marker List 219

Giant Beats and Giant Time display 220

Summary 221

14 MIXING YOUR PROJECT IN LOGIC PRO X

The goals of a mix 223

Volume 225

Panning 226

Balance versus panning 228

Working with FX plugins 232

Plugin categories 232

Managing FX plugins 235

Problem-solving with EQs 238

The Channel EQ 239

Controlling dynamics 241

Compressors 242

Limiters 243

Noise Gates 244

Modulation plugins 245

Delays 246

Reverbs 250

Mixing as you go versus starting from scratch 257

Other considerations 259

Summary 261

15 AUTOMATING YOUR MIX

A brief history of automation 263

Offline Region automation 266

Region panning automation 266

Plug-in bypass automation in a region 269

Live Track automation 270

Automation modes 270

Volume automation with Touch mode 271

Volume automation with Latch mode 272

Automatic lane creation with either Latch or Touch mode 274

Trimming automation 274

Real-time Trim 275

Copying automation 276

Copying automation within a
track 276

Copying automation between
tracks 277

The track automation Event List 277

Deleting automation 279

**Customizing MIDI controllers for
automation** 279

Summary 280

16 DELIVERING YOUR MUSIC FOR DISTRIBUTION

Bouncing a stereo mix 281

Opening the Bounce window 282

PCM file formats 285

MP3s and M4As 286

Realtime versus offline 287

**Exporting tracks to send to a mix
engineer** 288

Mastering your mix 288

The changed role of the
mastering engineer 289

Can you master your own tracks
in Logic Pro X? 289

Summary 292

INDEX 293

PREFACE

Logic Pro X is Apple's flagship application for music creation, found in many professional music studios across the globe. It is a powerful digital audio workstation that comes with all the software tools that you need to create music that sounds great. In the latest version, Logic Pro X 10.5, Apple has added impressive features to what was already a full package of tools, loops, FX plugins, and software instruments.

Providing a comprehensive introduction if you're new to Mac computer music creation, this practical guide will show you how to use Logic Pro X and have you up to speed in no time.

You'll not only understand what Apple's Logic Pro X software can do but also get hands-on with using it to accomplish various musical tasks. The book starts by getting you up and running with the basic terminologies. As you progress, you'll explore how to create audio and MIDI musical parts. To build on your knowledge further, the book will guide you through developing an automated mix. In addition to this, you'll learn how to bounce mixes and audio files for distribution.

By the end of this book, you'll be well-versed in Logic Pro X and have the skills you need to create professional-sounding music.

WHO THIS BOOK IS FOR

This book is for musicians, songwriters, and music producers who want to learn Logic Pro X from scratch with the help of expert guidance. A basic understanding of music theory, such as chords and notes, is helpful before you get started to get the most out of Logic Pro X and this book. This Apple Logic Pro X book also assumes that you'll be working on a Mac.

WHAT THIS BOOK COVERS

Chapter 1, Beginning with Logic Pro X 10.5, provides an overview of all the ways Logic Pro X can help you create music. It will give you an important understanding of what audio and MIDI actually are, what audio interfaces are and do, and which settings are global versus project-specific, with recommended settings.

Chapter 2, Getting to Know the Logic Pro X Interface, shows how easy it is to understand the interface, navigate it, and understand the basic terminology, meaning that, rather than being intimidated, new users will be confident that they can successfully learn how to use Logic Pro X.

Chapter 3, Recording Audio, introduces the good news that Logic Pro X gives you many ways to record and edit audio and MIDI. The bad news is that Logic Pro X gives you many ways to record and edit audio and MIDI. This chapter will guide you through the pros and cons of each so you can find your perfect workflow.

Chapter 4, Editing Audio, shows how to edit and use existing material to replace sections with the Marquee tool, how to choose the right Snap settings, and when audio editing is destructive versus non-destructive.

Chapter 5, Recording MIDI, demonstrates that creating music with Logic's vast array of virtual instruments is powerful and fun, once you understand how to use MIDI to make them shine. You will learn how to play in MIDI parts from a keyboard controller or the Musical Typing keyboard with software instruments and the different workflow options.

Chapter 6, Step Entering and Editing MIDI, shows how to step enter MIDI in the Piano Roll Editor to create parts. You will also learn how to refine the performance's timing, velocity, and other aspects of the MIDI performance.

Chapter 7, Logic Pro X's Drummer, shows that creating drum parts that sound like a real drummer or a drum machine for all genres is easy. Can't afford a real drummer or a bunch of vintage drum machines? No problem!

Chapter 8, Logic Pro X's Step Sequencer, introduces step sequencers – a feature of classic drum machines and modular synths and a long-requested feature for Logic Pro X. And now we have a great one!

Chapter 9, Working with Sampler, Quick Sampler, and Auto Sampler, explores how Logic Pro X's venerable EXS24 has received a major makeover and a **Quick Sampler** to boot, which is a gamechanger. Autosampler, previously only available in MainStage, is now also available in Logic Pro X.

Chapter 10, Working with Live Loops, discusses a concept made famous in Ableton Live that has also been incorporated into GarageBand for iOS. Now it is also incorporated into Logic Pro X.

Chapter 11, Working with Audio Files, Tempo, and Pitch, introduces Smart Tempo for ad-lib recording, Flex Time for fixing timing, and Flex Pitch for tuning your vocals – all exciting features in Logic Pro X. You will want to spend a lot of time with these.

Chapter 12, Getting the Arrangement Right, tackles the fact that if the arrangement isn't right, the end result will not have the impact you are seeking. This chapter will show you the author's favorite ways to get it right.

Chapter 13, Organizing for the Mix, addresses the fact that organization is essential – because an ounce of preparation is worth a pound of cure. Folder stacks, screensets, mixer naming, and its different views, as well as employing key commands and global tracks are all essential techniques for an efficient workflow that you will learn about.

Chapter 14, Mixing Your Project in Logic Pro X, covers how mixing is not about making everything sound great; it's about making it all work together. In this chapter, the author shares what he has learned on his own musical journey.

Chapter 15, Automating Your Mix, discusses the importance of giving your mix a sense of liveliness and breathing with automation. Offline or online? The author uses both at different times and explains the why and the how in this chapter. Virtually anything can be automated in Logic's plugins, as well as volume, panning, and muting. You will discover the difference it makes from just employing "set and forget."

Chapter 16, Delivering Your Music for Distribution, covers key aspects of distribution. Ever notice that commercial recordings sound pretty different from people's computer-based songs? Mastering is a big part of it. Do you need a mastering engineer? How do you send your mixes to another engineer or mastering engineer and finally out into the world? You will be led through all that in this final chapter.

TO GET THE MOST OUT OF THIS BOOK

You will need an Apple computer with macOS 10.14.6 or later and 6 GB of available storage space for the minimum installation or 72 GB of full Sound Library installation (recommended).

A rudimentary knowledge of basic music theory is assumed: note pitches and durations, key signatures, and so on. If you do not have that knowledge, you can still learn a lot, but it will limit you in certain chapters.

DOWNLOAD THE LOGIC PROJECT AND MEDIA FILES

You can also download the project files for the chapters:

1. Click on this link: https://github.com/PacktPublishing/Jumpstart-Logic-Pro-X-10.5

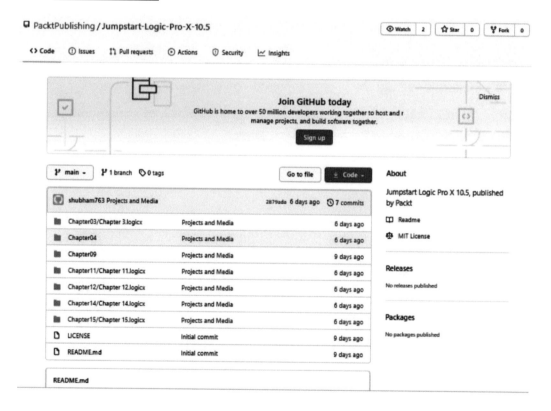

2. Click on **Code** and you should see the following dropdown menu:

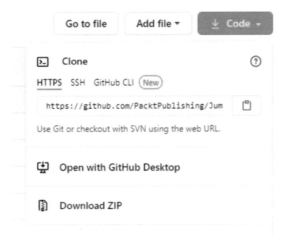

3. Select **Download Zip**. A zipped folder containing each chapter's project will be downloaded.

CONVENTIONS USED

There are a number of text conventions used throughout this book.

Bold: Indicates a new term, an important word, or words that you see onscreen. For example, words in menus or dialog boxes appear in the text like this. Here is an example: "Under the **Logic Pro X** menu, navigate to **Preferences | Advanced Tools**."

> TIPS OR IMPORTANT NOTES
> Appear like this.

GET IN TOUCH

Feedback from our readers is always welcome.

General feedback: If you have questions about any aspect of this book, mention the book title in the subject of your message and email us at customercare@packtpub.com.

Errata: Although we have taken every care to ensure the accuracy of our content, mistakes do happen. If you have found a mistake in this book, we would be grateful if you would report this to us. Please visit www.packtpub.com/support/errata, selecting your book, clicking on the Errata Submission Form link, and entering the details.

Piracy: If you come across any illegal copies of our works in any form on the Internet, we would be grateful if you would provide us with the location address or website name. Please contact us at copyright@packt.com with a link to the material.

REVIEWS

Please leave a review. Once you have read and used this book, why not leave a review on the site that you purchased it from? Potential readers can then see and use your unbiased opinion to make purchase decisions, we at Packt can understand what you think about our products, and our authors can see your feedback on their book. Thank you!

For more information about Packt, please visit packt.com.

1 BEGINNING WITH LOGIC PRO X 10.5

If you have purchased this book, then you probably already know that Logic Pro X is Apple's flagship application for music creation. I like to say that if you can conceive it, you can create it with Logic Pro X 10.5. It comes with everything you really need, and more, at a bargain price.

10.5 has added some very impressive features to what was already a full package of tools, loops, FX plug-ins, and software instruments. In addition to Logic Pro X's revolutionary Drummer, Drum Machine Designer has had a significant upgrade and works with Live Loops in an exciting way that Ableton Live and GarageBand iOS users will be familiar with. Quick Sampler, along with the new updated Sampler, is a game changer for me. Auto Sampler, previously only available in Main Stage, is now part of Logic Pro X. Recording your vocals and guitars is now a snap.

Specifically, this chapter covers the following topics:

- Important information for beginning with Logic Pro X 10.5
- Audio versus MIDI
- What hardware besides my Mac will I need?
- Preferences versus Project Settings

IMPORTANT INFORMATION FOR BEGINNING WITH LOGIC PRO X

You know the old saying "an ounce of prevention is worth a pound of cure"? In this chapter, you will learn all you need to begin your Logic Pro X journey.

WHAT ARE AUDIO AND MIDI?

In this section, we will look at the differences between Audio and MIDI.

When you record yourself singing or playing a real instrument in Logic Pro X, the truth is you are actually recording an audio waveform to a drive with Logic Pro X as a conduit. If you delete Logic Pro X from your computer, your recording will still be there, unless you delete it.

I like to compare it to a house: somebody drew up a blueprint, ordered the supplies, and built the house.

Musical Instrument Digital Interface (MIDI) is just a set of instructions that is interpreted by a software instrument, synthesizer, or other hardware keyboard that is capable of understanding it. For example, when you press a key on a keyboard controller, Logic sees "sound this note that we agree is middle C, play it this loud, hold it for this length of time."

If you load a flute sound in a software instrument, you hear what sounds like a flute. If you load a piano sound, it sounds like a piano. If you record a part and then delete it, it's gone and if you don't save the project, it's gone when you quit Logic. Unlike an audio file, which is a waveform recorded on a hard drive, a MIDI region is just a set of instructions that are saved in the Logic project.

So, it's more like the blueprint for the house than the constructed house.

SELECTING ESSENTIAL HARDWARE FOR LOGIC PRO X 10.5

As well as a Mac, you may need some additional hardware to effectively use Logic Pro X. Let's explore what we can add to our setup.

AN AUDIO INTERFACE

While most Mac computers have a built-in microphone audio playback capability, and a speaker, they are not really adequate for creating good-sounding music, just for perhaps getting ideas down.

When you want to use a microphone to record your voice singing or speaking, your computer needs something to record it. Firstly, the microphone won't be loud enough, so you need a microphone pre-amp (mic pre). An audio interface will have one or more of these.

Also, microphones are analog devices and computers don't understand analog information unless it is translated to digital information. So, you need an analog-to-digital converter. Then, for the sound to go back out to speakers, which 99% of the time are analog, you need a digital-to-analog converter. An audio interface will have these.

You need one or more inputs to plug your microphones or instrument cables into, and outputs to a set of speakers or a console. You will often see the inputs and outputs referred to as I/O. You'll also require a headphone jack to listen through headphones.

I now have some good news for you. It used to be that to buy an audio interface that had one or more good mic pres and good converters, you had to spend a fair amount of money. Now it is hard to buy one that doesn't have those. Mostly, the more expensive ones will have more ins and outs, which you might need to record a whole band or mic a drum set with multiple mics. For most of you, however, one or two mic pres and ins with a stereo output will be just fine. There are even USB microphones that include an audio interface that podcasters frequently turn to.

Speaking of microphones, if you are singer or want to record a saxophone or other instrument that does not plug in to the audio interface directly with a cable, you will need a microphone or two. Again, they range from the inexpensive but decent to the incredibly expensive. There are essentially three kinds of microphones: condenser, dynamic, and ribbon mics:

- **Condenser mics** are commonly used to record vocals and acoustic instruments. They feature an extended and flat frequency range and come with either large or small capsules. They are less commonly used on live stages because they pick up more off-axis sounds, may not handle really loud signals coming into them as well as dynamic mics do, and they are less durable. Also, they require phantom power, which is built into most mixers and mic pres. The Neumann U47 and U87 are two famous examples. The price ranges from very inexpensive to *really* expensive.

- **Dynamic mics**, like the famous Shure SM57 and 58 that you see, are widely used on stage because they do reject off-axis sound, can handle really loud signals, and if you drop them, they probably will not break. Also, they are generally pretty inexpensive. They also are widely used in studios, even though they have a less extended frequency range, color the sound, and are less detailed. But for miking guitar amps and rap and screaming rock vocals, they may still be your choice.

- **Ribbon mics** were probably the most common mics in recording studios from the 1930s until the 1970s but fell out of favor when high-quality condenser mics became more prevalent. In recent years, they have become more popular again. They are usually fairly expensive, although less expensive ones have appeared in the marketplace. The classic diamond-shaped ribbon mic is associated with Frank Sinatra. Modern-day offerings from companies like RØDE and Royer Labs have now become popular.

I will only say that the microphone type and costliness don't always determine how well it pairs with your voice. I recorded all the vocals on my album *Honestly* (I know, shameless self-promotion) with a $400 dynamic mic.

You can, of course, delay any decision and use the built-in capabilities of your Mac until you get your feet wet, if you wish.

A MIDI CONTROLLER

These can consist of a wide combination of keys, knobs, faders, and drum pads. If you are a real pianist, you might want one with 88 full-size weighted keys. If you aren't, 37 unweighted small keys may be fine. If you are not going to play much in real time but just program the information in, then Logic's built-in virtual keyboard may be sufficient. There are decent inexpensive ones and then more expensive ones, depending on your needs.

MONITOR SPEAKERS

Unlike the speakers you listen to music on for pleasure, these are not designed to make the music sound as good as possible but are designed to be "flat" so that you can be pretty sure that it translates well, meaning that the mix you hear will be approximately the way it will sound in most people's listening environments. There is a huge range of price and size configurations, from nearfield, to midfield, to larger speaker systems with sub-woofers. For most music creators, a decent pair of nearfields gets the job done. Also, the room you are in plays a role as it may be too dead sounding, too reflective, or trap bass frequencies, and that affects what you hear when you are listening to your music and mixing it.

So, if your room is not treated or good sounding, can you mix just with headphones and forgo speakers? Yes, but there are disadvantages that I will discuss when we deal with mixing.

MONITOR HEADPHONES

Again, these are not about beautiful sound but accurate reproduction. As is the case with monitors, you want the headphones to give you as uncolored a sound as possible so that you know how your music will sound on other systems.

Enough talk about gear, let's talk about Logic Pro X and all that you will derive from learning to use it well.

PREFERENCES VERSUS PROJECT SETTINGS

A **Preference** in Logic will affect every Logic project past, present, and future, starting from choices you make after you open it for the very first time.

Project Settings are specific to a given project and therefore do not necessarily affect past or future projects, unless they are saved in a template. There are ways, however, to create defaults that you can apply to past or present projects, as you will learn.

Over the following sections, we'll explore how to use preferences and project settings when you are opening Logic Pro X for the first time.

OPENING LOGIC PRO X FOR THE VERY FIRST TIME!

If you have already opened Logic before, you have seen this in the past and may be getting different behavior. By default, Logic looks for your most recently opened project. If this truly is the first time you have opened it, you may see a description of **What's New** in the Logic version you are opening. Following that, this is what you will see:

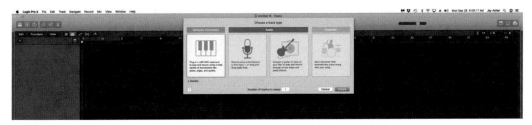

Figure 1.1: Creating tracks in a new project

Everything flows through **Channel Strips** in Logic, some for creating MIDI parts with software instruments, others for recording audio, and then there is Logic's amazing

Drummer, which we will cover in *Chapter 7, Logic Pro X's Drummer*. To proceed, you need to create at least one Channel Strip.

Opening the **Details** arrow gives you more information and options:

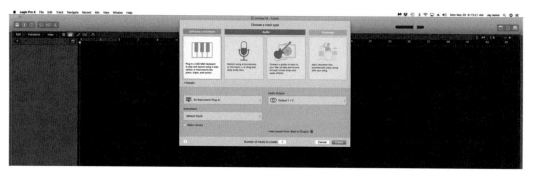

Figure 1.2: Selecting a track type

I decide to go with an Audio Channel Strip without opening the Library, for now. My first Logic project is now open. The following figure shows my open project, with the added Audio Channel Strip track:

Figure 1.3: A new Logic project with one audio track

If, like most new users of Logic Pro X, you first started with GarageBand, boy doesn't this look familiar?

Yes, it does, and that is because they are both the creations of the same design team!

But we want Logic Pro X, not GarageBand, so we will use the Preferences to do just that. Because they are Preferences, we will only need to do it once. If you are familiar with *Superman*, either the comic strips, TV shows, or movies, you know that he is mild-mannered Clark Kent until he goes into a phone booth, rips off his clothes and glasses, and becomes Superman. This our Superman moment!

Under the **Logic Pro X** menu, navigate to **Preferences | Advanced Tools**:

Figure 1.4: Advanced Tools Preferences

Click on **Show Advanced Tools** and you will see that you can enable a selection of them or enable all of them. You will want to check **Enable All**, but then uncheck **Surround**, unless you are already set up for surround sound with your speaker system.

Click the red dot at the top to exit the **Advanced Tools** window and, as you can see, the look of the interface has changed a bit. *Congratulations*, you are now seeing Logic Pro X.

CHANGING LOGIC PRO X'S DEFAULT OPENING BEHAVIOR

As I said, by default, Logic will look to open the most recent project you are working on, and that is fine if that is what you choose, but I don't recommend it. First of all, I think most users work on more than one project at a time. Secondly, projects *can* get corrupted and have trouble opening. Although that is rare and there are strategies to deal with it, I prefer not to have it be my default.

Let's explore the other options.

Under the **Logic Pro X** menu, navigate to **Preferences | General**.

In the **Project Handling** tab, if you hold down on **Startup Action** you see the choices you have:

- **Do Nothing**: Just what it sounds like. Logic looks for a further choice from you.
- **Open Most Recent Project**: The default.
- **Open Existing Project**: Logic will open the default save location and let you look for a specific project.
- **Select a Template**: Logic comes with several templates and you can create your own.
- **Create New Empty Project**: Self-explanatory, I think.
- **Create New Project Using Default Template**: Fine if you only use one.
- **Ask**: This is my recommended choice, for two reasons. The first is sometimes I

want a specific template, sometimes I want a specific project, and sometimes I want to start from scratch. I like options. Secondly, how often does anyone ask me what I truly want? (**sniffle**)

Whichever you choose, that will be the default unless you go back and change it, and if you quit Logic and then re-open it, that is the behavior you will get. Your choices may change over time and I am not the workflow police if you have a different preference, but for me, **Ask** is the way to go.

SUMMARY

You have now been introduced to the concepts of audio and MIDI, and how they differ. You own a Mac and Logic Pro X but there is additional hardware that you will want to have to use it effectively. The good news is that it doesn't have to be expensive. You now understand that Logic Pro X has both Preferences, which affect all projects, and Project Settings, which are project specific, although some can be saved as defaults. You have learned your choices as to how Logic Pro X behaves when opening it, and my personal preference.

In the next chapter, we will become familiar with all the areas in the Logic Pro X interface, along with its menus and its terminology. You will learn about how to set Tools in each window, and all the vast content that comes as part of Logic Pro X, including sounds and Apple Loops that you can load from the Library.

2 GETTING TO KNOW THE LOGIC PRO X INTERFACE

Part of learning to effectively use any software is to have a clear understanding of its interface and its terminology, and this is especially true with powerful software such as Logic Pro X. Also, Logic Pro X comes with a ton of content that you will find in both the Library and the Loop Browser. Once you have gained a solid understanding of it, you will be on your way to a great time creating music with Logic Pro X.

This chapter consists of the following main topics:

- Logic Pro X windows, menus, and terminology
- The Logic Pro X Library
- The Browser
- Apple Loops and the Loop Browser

LOGIC PRO X WINDOWS, MENUS, AND TERMINOLOGY

We will begin by explaining the Logic Pro windows, exploring its menus, and mastering its terminology so that we are clear on what we are discussing as we learn to use Logic Pro X.

THE MAIN WINDOW

Shockingly the main window you see when you open a new Logic Pro X project is called ... wait for it ... **the Main Window**!

You may hear some long-time Logic Pro users refer to it as the Arrange window because for many, many years that was indeed what the window was named.

Most of what you need to do in Logic Pro X can indeed be done in only this window, but as you will learn, there are other options. By default, **Quick Help** will be turned on and it is very helpful for beginners.

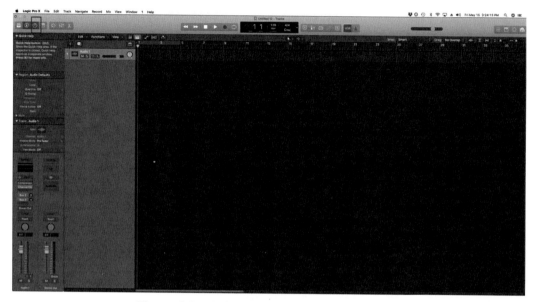

Figure 2.1 – Quick Help in the Main Window

You can toggle it on/off by clicking the question mark button in the top left of the **Control bar**, which is the light gray area running across the Graphical User Interface of the Main Window, hereafter referred to as the **GUI**. As you hold your mouse or trackpad down on each button, **Quick Help** will tell you what it is. I recommend that you click each one and see how they behave when toggled on and off.

> **IMPORTANT NOTE**
>
> If when you open a new project, your only track creation option is **External MIDI**, then create that. The problem is that Logic Pro cannot see an audio interface. If you do not have one hooked up, Logic Pro should default to your built-in audio with a laptop or iMac. If it isn't seeing that or your audio interface, go under the **Logic Pro X** menu to **Preferences | Audio** and in the **Devices** tab, select the audio interface or built-in options and click **Apply Changes**. Don't worry about the other settings for now.

The Control bar is one of the three main areas of the Main Window and it is very important to your workflow and extremely customizable, which will be especially helpful for laptop users who are screen real estate challenged.

Directly below the Control bar is the **Bar Ruler**, which displays bars and beats. The vertical white line you see is called the **Playhead** and if you press the play button, you will see it start to move throughout the project until you press the stop button. Pressing the rewind button brings you back to the beginning.

Below the bar ruler is the second important area in the main window, the **Tracks area**. It contains the **Track List** and the grid where you will record and edit all your regions, called the Tracks Area (although the Quick Help refers to it as the Workspace.)

On the left side of the GUI, you see the third important area – it's called the **Inspector**.

If you have Quick Help toggled on, you will see an area at the top with the description **Quick Help**. You will also see a disclosure triangle that closes it.

Below it is the part of the Inspector that affects the region, called the **Region Inspector**. Settings there will affect any regions you select, whether they are on the same track or different tracks. It too has a disclosure triangle to close it, but also another to show more within it.

The next area in the Inspector has settings that control the entire track and is called the **Track Inspector**.

Below that are two faders, similar to what you might see on a recording console. The one on the left pertains to the Channel Strip of the selected track while the one on the right of it shows the Stereo Output, where all signal goes to if you are working "in the box" and then going out of your audio interface with outputs going to hardware mixers, or a tape recorder, or another hardware device.

TRACKS VERSUS CHANNEL STRIPS

There is some Logic Pro X terminology that often confuses newcomers, and for a very good reason – it *is* confusing.

I will now create a second track either by clicking the **+** at the top of the track list or by navigating to the **Track** menu and choosing **New Tracks…**. As before, we see choices for creating new tracks:

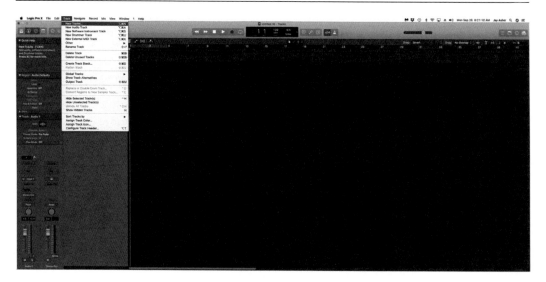

Figure 2.2 – Creating new tracks

The truth is, we are creating tracks, but we are also creating channel strips, each with a single track flowing through it. But it is possible to have multiple tracks flowing through the same channel strip, and there are times that you will want to.

For now, create a **Software Instrument track** with Details showing. Create it as an Empty Channel Strip with **Open Library** checked.

> NOTE
>
> In addition to the choices of **Audio**, **Software Instrument**, and **Drummer** tracks, you also will see **External MIDI** and **Guitar** or **Bass**. External MIDI is for recording sounds from a keyboard or tone module while Guitar or Bass is actually also an audio track with different plugin choices.

Next, we will examine the Library in Logic Pro X, where we find helpful combinations of Software Instruments and FX plugins.

THE LOGIC PRO X LIBRARY

The **Library** has a collection of already created **patches**. A patch is a collection of plugins designed to help you achieve a certain sound. You can also create your own and save them to the library.

The Library's visible content is related to the kind of channel strip you choose in the Track List. If it's an Audio channel strip, you will see various kinds of FX plugins. If it is a Software Instrument channel strip, you will see Software Instrument and FX plugin combinations. If it's a Drummer channel strip, you will see drummers and drum kits:

1. Select the Audio track and see the choices.

2. Then select the Software Instrument track and notice that they change. If you select a patch in the Library, it will automatically load the plugins to the channel strip.

3. With the Software Instrument track selected in the Track List, select the **Steinway Grand Piano** patch and you will see that it loads Logic Pro X's Sampler software instrument (before 10.5, it was called EXS 24) and an EQ, Compressor, and a Tape Delay. There are also two **Sends**. The sends control the level being sent to two busses, each assigned as the input on an aux, that have reverbs instantiated on them. Don't worry if you don't understand what all those are and do. I will teach you about them when we get to learn about mixing in *Chapter 13, Organizing for the Mix*.

4. If you have a MIDI controller hooked up to your computer, you will be able to play notes and hear the sound. If not, press **Command + K** to open a virtual keyboard. Play notes on it and in the **LCD** section of the Control bar, you will see a little dot appear that shows that it is receiving MIDI input.

5. You can now close the Library. There are two ways to do so. You can click the **Library** button on the Control bar or simply press the letter **Y** on your computer keyboard.

Congratulations, you have just learned your first key command. I will be showing you some more, and I encourage you to keep a list or memorize them. My personal motto is "never do by dragging the mouse or trackpad around what you can do with a keystroke."

While we are at it, press the letter *I* and notice that you can toggle the Inspector open and hidden.

If those do not work, then the key command sets are not assigned properly. They should be set correctly by default but I occasionally have seen Logic default to a Pro Tools compatible set seemingly for no reason.

> **IMPORTANT NOTE**
>
> If the key commands are not working, go to the **Logic Pro X** menu to **Key Commands | Presets** and choose the ones appropriate for your language.

THE TOOLBAR

If you either click the Toolbar button on the Control bar or under the LCD display, grab the blue line, and drag down, you will see the Toolbar. When Logic Pro went from Logic Pro 9 to Logic Pro X, the whole paradigm of the Toolbar was changed into the present Control bar, so the Toolbar has been deemphasized in Logic Pro X. Many users still find it useful, and like the Control bar, it is customizable:

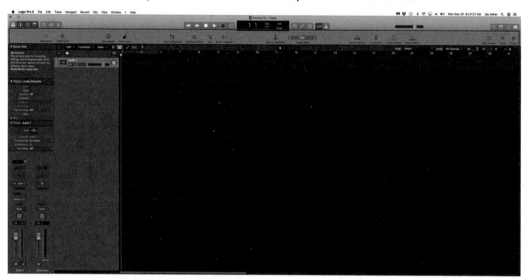

Figure 2.3 – Logic Pro X Toolbar

CUSTOMIZING THE CONTROL BAR AND TOOLBAR

If you are using a laptop with a small display, it is entirely possible that you will not see everything included by default and will see some arrows that you can hold down on to see more. Even on a large display or two displays, however, the default is not optimal for working with Logic Pro X in my opinion, so I will show you how to customize it to your specific needs now.

On the right side of the LCD in the center of the Control bar, if you hold down your mouse or trackpad, you will see some options for the Control bar display:

Figure 2.4 – Control bar display options

1. Choose **Customize Control bar and Display**.

2. Hold down your mouse or trackpad and change from **Beats & Project** to **Custom**, and wow – you will see it has changed greatly. On a small screen, you see even less!

No worries, this is where customizing is powerful. Look at the default **Views** that are checked:

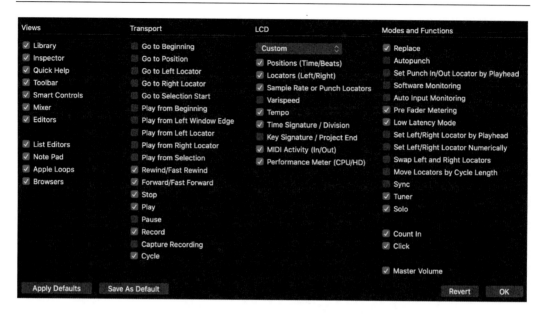

Figure 2.5 – Selected default Views

If you memorize the relevant key commands, most of these are unnecessary. In fact, I have already mentioned a couple, but now I will give you a list:

- **Y** toggles the **Library**.
- **I** toggles the **Inspector**
- **Left Shift + forward slash** toggles **Quick Help**.
- **Control + Option + Command + T** toggles the **Toolbar**.
- **B** toggles the **Smart Controls**.
- **X** toggles the **Mixer**
- **E** toggles the **Editors**.
- **D** toggles the **List Editors**.
- **Option + Command + P** toggles the **Note Pad**.
- **O** toggles the **Loop Browser**.
- **F** toggles the **File Browser**.

If you memorize some or all of these, you can uncheck them here and free up space in the Control bar. I recommend that you uncheck all but the more complicated ones.

Under the **Transport** menu, you can check or uncheck what you would like to see. Since I know that the spacebar puts Logic Pro into play mode, while pressing it again stops playback, and the **Enter** key returns to the beginning, I don't need many of these, but for you, you may feel more comfortable leaving it as it is.

Under **LCD**, notice that I have checked **Sample Rate or Punch Locators**. When we visit audio recording in the next chapter, you will understand why. I have also made some changes that suit me in **Modes and Functions**, but frankly, I change these often.

Once you have made your choices, you can then click **Save As Default**. While these are Project Settings and not Preferences, they are not global to Logic, but they will now ensure that every new Logic project will default to them. When you open an earlier Logic project, if you open your customizing window again, you can choose **Apply Defaults** and then resave the project.

Right-clicking or clicking on the Toolbar while holding the **Control** key gives you a similar menu of choices to what you see on the Toolbar. I rarely use the Toolbar so I have no specific recommendations, but you may reach a very different conclusion and that is fine.

LOGIC PRO X'S INCLUDED CONTENT

Logic comes with a ton of content, including software instruments, FX, and Apple loops. You will want to make sure you have downloaded it all to your main hard drive. Later, you can move the content to another drive quite easily (you will see **Relocate Sound Library...** in the following screenshot):

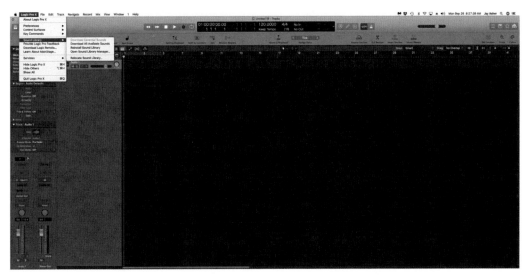

Figure 2.6 – Opening Sound Library to download content

If you choose **Open Sound Library Manager...**, you will see whether they are all installed. If not, choose **Select all unfinished** and they will download. You will see a thin blue progress bar below the Control bar. You can download in the background while you continue to work in Logic Pro X.

The Browser is the area where you can see audio files that are in your project, in other projects, and in iTunes or your Movies folder.

EXPLORING THE BROWSER

There are three browsers that are included: the Project Browser, the Media Browser, and the All Files browser.

You open the Browser by clicking the icon in the Control bar or by pressing the letter **F** on your computer keyboard.

> NOTE
> Some of this may be a little over your head at this point but don't worry. You can always come back and review it later when you are more comfortable with Logic Pro, but since it is one of the main areas in Logic, I feel it is important to explain the Browser to you.

THE PROJECT BROWSER

The Project Browser shows you your project audio without the necessity of opening the Project Audio window:

Figure 2.7 – The Project Browser

In this window, it is easy to drag audio files into the workspace that are not in the workspace. Select **Used** or **Unused** to see which are in the workspace and which are not, or delete those you are not using.

THE MEDIA BROWSER

This browser provides you with a view of music in the music app or movies you have so that you can import them into your project. I hardly ever use it, frankly:

Figure 2.8 – The Media Browser

THE ALL FILES BROWSER

There are three buttons at the top: **Computer, Home, and Project**. In the following screenshot, **Computer** is chosen:

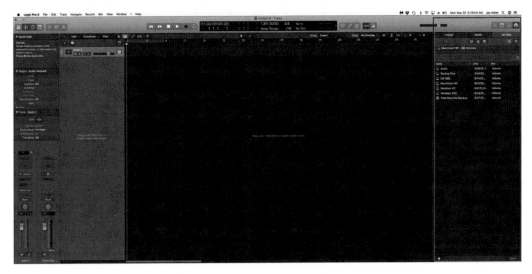

Figure 2.9 – The All FIles Browser

In the **Computer** view, you see all your storage devices to search for files you might want to add to your project.

The **Home** button shows the contents of your home directory.

The **Project** button shows all the projects in your Project folder, which is where Logic Pro saves projects by default. This is the most useful browser area in my opinion, as it allows you to import Global settings, tracks, and content.

When you select a project in this window, you can click on **Import Project Settings** at the bottom-right of the window and you then have the ability to choose exactly what you wish to import into your project. With the tabs at the top, you can filter what you wish to see, for greater ease of viewing. There is a slider at the bottom that allows you to see more things you can import, such as **Sends**:

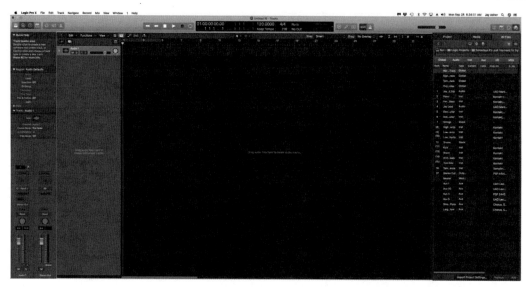

Figure 2.10 – Importing from another project into the All Files Browser

We'll explore how we can use Apple loops in the next section.

APPLE LOOPS AND THE LOOP BROWSER

The Loop Browser is where you will find a massive bunch of royalty-free Apple Loops that you may use in your musical projects. You probably have heard many of them already. If, for instance, you have heard Rihanna's big hit "*Umbrella,*" you have heard Apple Loops on a commercial recording.

Apple loops have the virtue of adapting to any tempo or key. There are Audio loops, Software Instrument loops, Drummer loops, and 10.5 Pattern loops.

You can open the Loop Browser by clicking on the button that looks like a loop on the right-hand side of the Control bar, but heck, why not just press the letter **O**?

Logic defaults to a tempo of 120 beats per minute (bpm) and the key of C major. Loops are categorized by Instruments, Genre, Descriptors, and even Moods. You won't see Moods in the default Button view but if you click on the icon next to it, it changes to Column view, and then you do. You can also tag some as Favorites. You can sort them by name (the default) or the number of beats, or tempo, or key, just by clicking on any one of those above the loops list. There are also loop packs that you can access by holding the mouse or trackpad down where you see All Packs.

You can also view or hide specific types of loops from view:

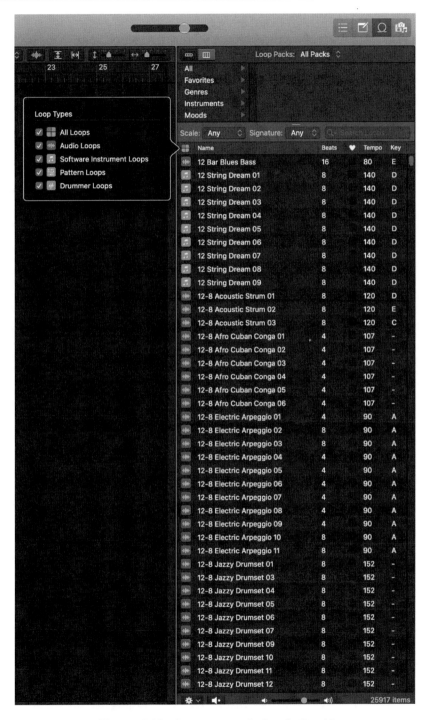

Figure 2.11 – Loop types in Logic Pro X

Let's have some fun, shall we?

1. Click on **Instrument | All Drums**.
2. Click on **Genre** and choose **Modern R&B**.
3. Click on **Descriptors** and choose **Single**, **Processed**, and **Grooving**.

We have narrowed down the choices a bit. You can listen to a loop to audition it just by clicking on it, and you will hear it at the tempo, and key if it is melodic or harmonic, of the Logic project. I kind of dig **Light The Fuse Beat 01**. I see that it is an Audio loop because of the blue wave symbol, that it is four measures long (16 beats), and that was originally at 140 bpm, but it sounds fine at 120.

If I drag it to the workspace below the two already existing tracks, it will create an audio track, but since we already have one, I will drag it to that. Look at what we see as we do so. The numbers tell us the position in the timeline we are dragging it to and its length. If we position it right at the beginning, it is at 1 1 1 1. What does that mean?

The first number is the bar. The second number is the beat (a quarter note in 4/4) and the third number is the sixteenth note in the quarter note. The last number is ticks. There are 240 ticks per sixteenth note. So, this is positioned at the first bar, first beat, the first sixteenth in the beat, and the first tick. The length is 4 0 0 0, four bars long. If it were 4 ½, it would read 4 2 0 0.

Notice that when we drag it in, it changes the Logic project tempo to 140 bpm. If we either pull down on 140 in the LCD, until we reach 120, or better yet, double-click on it and type 120, we are back to 120 bpm. Let's decide on 130 and, as you hear, the loop chases the tempo perfectly.

A good start, but now we want other loops to play with it. To audition them while hearing this one, we want to create a four-bar cycle. We can simply drag our mouse or trackpad in the bar ruler from bar 1 to bar 5 and create it, and when we hit play, it will continuously repeat those four bars, with the Playhead never advancing past bar 5. But that is not as easy as simply selecting the region and pressing the **U** key to set the cycle by the region locators.

Now let's add bass with the following steps:

1. In the Loop Browser, click the **X** to reset it.
2. Choose **Instrument, Bass**, then **Genre Modern R&B**, and **Descriptors Single, Processed**, and **Grooving**.
3. Either press the Play button in the Transport in the Control bar or press the spacebar on the computer keyboard, and it begins to play the beat loop over and over.

4. Select **Loops** in the Loop Browser to hear how they sound with the beat loop until you hear a loop you like.

Flip The Switch Bass works for me. Try to drag it to the Software Instrument track that already exists, and you get a warning that it isn't an Audio track and that green Apple loops, not blue Apple loops, work on those. No problem – just drag it into the workspace below the other two tracks and it creates a track for you.

Play and listen, and it's already pretty cool.

Maybe we now want an electric guitar, but when we use the same genre and descriptors, we may conclude that we are not finding any that work with the existing material to our satisfaction. But we are creative people, so go to the Loop Pack called **Chillwave**, and select **Guitars** and audition some, and sure enough, there is one that I like, called **Digital Riff Guitar**. It was originally in the key of D major and we are in C major – not very far from the original, which means that it should sound pretty good, and I think it does. (If you don't, choose another.)

Into the workspace, below the others, it goes. It is, however, only 8 beats long, not 16 like the others. So now we'll learn about looping, which is different than cycling.

Let's explore looping techniques:

1. Press **C** to turn off the cycle.

2. Drag over all three loops with the mouse or trackpad (this is known as rubber-banding) or press **Command + A**, which in most Apple applications is Select All and all the regions are selected.

3. In the Region Inspector, you will see **3 selected** and if you check the **Loop** checkbox, they will all loop for the length of the project. Alternatively, when they are selected, just press **L**.

In this manner, I can continue to add Apple loops to my heart's content.

At this point, you may well have decided that this project is a keeper and you don't want to run the risk of losing your work. The *most* important thing in creating music on a computer is... **saving your project!**

SAVING YOUR PROJECT

Press **Command + S**, or go to the **File** menu and choose **Save As**. You can save your project either as a GarageBand style package, where any of the files you save with it are embedded, or as a Folder, which will have separate sub-folders. Normally, I prefer the latter, but because I don't need to check any of those as we are only using Loop Browser loops, I will choose Package with all those unchecked.

Whew, glad we did that! Now let's work some more with what we have. It's time to learn about our Main Window tools.

THE LEFT-CLICK AND COMMAND-CLICK TOOLS

The **Left-click tool** is the primary tool and it defaults to the Pointer tool, but as you can see in this screenshot, it can be assigned to any of a number of different tools:

Figure 2.12: The Left-click Tool

The Pointer tool can behave differently depending on where in the region you position it.

Here are some examples that will illustrate the behaviors:

1. Select the **Steinway Grand Piano** track and press **delete** or hold the Track Header, and it turns into a hand, and to the left and it goes – poof!

2. Select the three regions and press **L** to turn off looping.

3. Select the bass and guitar regions, and while keeping an eye on the help tag, drag them to begin at bar 3.

4. Select all three again and if you position the Pointer tool in the upper-right corner of the regions, it turns into the Loop tool. You can then drag them to the right to end at bar 15.

5. But the bass was longer than the guitar, so it extends an extra two bars. No problem. Click in an empty area of the workspace to deselect the regions.

6. Position the Pointer on the bass region at bar 15, where it turns into the Loop tool, and just press down.

I'm loving it, but I think I would like to have the bass play the last three notes of the loop to lead into its entrance. This is where we can use the **Command-click tool**.

It defaults to the Marquee tool, but like the Left-click tool, it can be assigned to any one of the others.

This is the most useful tool for moving or copying sections of a region. Let's see how it can work for us:

1. With the bass region selected, press **L** to turn off the loop.

2. Press **Z** for zoom to fit selection and then press **S** to solo it, or press the **S** in the track header.

3. Hold the **Command** key and notice that the Pointer tool turns into the Marquee tool. Now drag it over the last three notes of the bass region and press the spacebar to hear it.

That will work great. If I press down with the mouse, it splits the region so that the last three notes are now a separate region. I want to copy it to the right place, but I want to be precise, and the **Snap** menu can be set to help me.

SNAP

If I hold down on the **Snap** menu, I have a lot of choices as to the behavior when I copy a region:

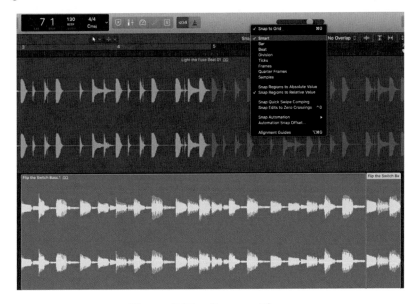

Figure 2.13 – Snap settings

My newly created region is at 6 3 3 1, so exactly at the third beat and third sixteenth note of the beat. So, if we want to snap to a division, an eighth note in this instance, and exactly on the division, an absolute value is the right choice. Follow these steps to achieve this:

1. Press **S** to turn off Solo.

2. Set the **Snap** settings to those I described.

3. While holding the **Option** key, drag the new bass region to 2 3 3 1, remembering to first release the mouse or trackpad before releasing the **Option** key. Otherwise, you will move it, rather than copying it.

4. You now have three bass regions. Select the last two and press **Command + J** to merge them.

5. Select the merged region and position the Pointer tool so that it becomes the Loop tool and loop until bar 15 again.

Play it and wow – it's really getting somewhere. But I want to hear the bass more clearly when it enters. Again, the Marquee tool is my friend and it's time to introduce you to my favorite key command!

If you press the forward slash key next to the right **Shift** key, it opens up the **Go To Position** dialog box. To go to the place in the timeline where the bass now enters, type *2*, press the spacebar, type *3*, press the spacebar, and either type *1* or leave it alone since it defaults to 1 tick. Press **OK**, or the **Return** key and the Playhead advances to that position. This is my favorite way to go precisely to any place in my project.

Now that the Playhead is exactly where we want it, we can use the Marquee tool to delete or mute part of the region:

1. Hold the **Command** key so that the Marquee tool appears and drag it over the beat region from 2 3 3 1 to 3 1 1 1.

2. Either press **delete** or **Control + M** to mute it – your choice.

Press **Command + S** to save your work.

CHANGING THE KEY AND TRANSPOSING REGIONS

I am singing along with this, improvising, and it feels just a little low to me. I wish it were in Db major rather than C major.

These are Apple loops, so no problem, right? In the top right of the Control bar, the first button opens the **List Editors**. Or, I can simply press *D*. I want the **Signature** tab.

Sure enough, I see that it is in 4/4 and the key of C major, as expected. I hold down the mouse or trackpad and change it to Db major and voila – when I hit play, it's in the key I want.

Maybe though I want to start in C and modulate up to Db. To achieve this, you can follow these steps:

1. In the **Signature** list editor, I go back to C Major and exit the **Signature** list editor.

2. Using the **Go To Position** key command, I set the Playhead to bar 7.

3. With the bass and guitar regions selected, I either go to the **Edit** menu in the main menus and choose **Split | Regions at Playhead** or better yet, press **Command + T**.

4. With the two newly created regions that begin at bar 7 selected, in the **Region Inspector** next to the word **Transpose**, I either drag up or double-click and type *+1*.

When I play my project back, sure enough, I hear the regions playing in the key of C and then at bar 7, modulating up a half step to Db major.

Remember to save your project now!

SUMMARY

You have now been introduced to the three main areas of the main window. The Control bar and Toolbar are important for your workflow, and you can customize them greatly. You have learned about the Library and its Channel Strip settings. Hopefully, you enjoyed choosing Apple loops from the Loop Browser. As you now know, the **Snap** setting and Left-click and Command-click tool choices are critical to what you are trying to accomplish in the workspace. Changing the key in Logic Pro X can be done in the Signature List and Transposing regions, in the Region Inspector.

In *Chapter 3, Recording Audio*, we will become familiar with considerations for preparing for recording audio. You will explore the many workflow choices to record audio in Logic Pro X and the advantages of each. You will learn how to then improve a recording by adding takes and punching in and out automatically or manually. Also, you will learn the value of having alternative versions of a project and saving a project as a template.

3 RECORDING AUDIO

The good news is that Logic Pro X gives you a bunch of ways to record audio, using your voice, guitar, saxophone, or any other "real" source. The bad news is that Logic Pro X gives you a bunch of ways to record audio, like your voice, guitar, saxophone, or any other "real" source. Seriously though, there are advantages to each method, and you may very well take advantage of several different workflows.

Specifically, this chapter covers the following topics:

- The Project Templates
- Setting Preferences
- Project settings
- Cycle recording options
- Recording without cycling
- Saving a template

This is the first chapter in which you will want to use one of my projects that I have provided for you, `Chapter 3.logicx`. For now, though, let's begin by opening one of the included templates.

> NOTE:
> The project and media files for the chapters are available at this link, https://github.com/PacktPublishing/Jumpstart-Logic-Pro-X-10.5
> Instructions on how to download the files are added in the preface.

THE PROJECT TEMPLATES

If you have set your default action for opening Logic to **Ask**, as I suggested in *Chapter 1, Beginning with Logic Pro X 10.5.* you will see you have the option of **New from Template**. In **Project Templates**, you see **Hip Hop**, **Electronic**, **Songwriter**, **Orchestral**, **Multi-Track**, and **Music for Picture**. Each has a description and if you open the **Details** disclosure triangle, you see even more options to tweak before you open it:

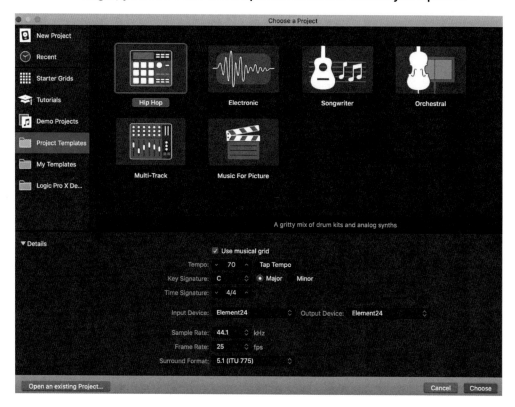

Figure 3.1 – Project Templates

I recommend you eventually take the time to explore all the templates. I think for teaching you about recording audio, Songwriter is the way to go:

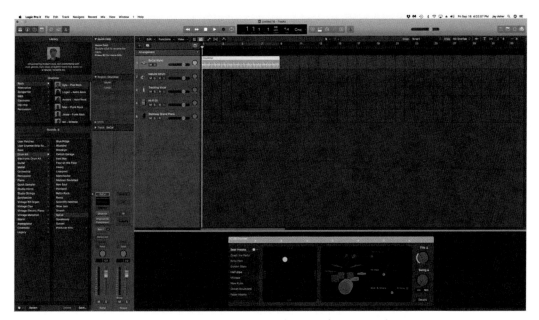

Figure 3.2 – The Songwriter project template

As you can see, the template creates a Drummer track with a Drummer region, a sampler software instrument with a **Steinway Grand Piano** sound, three audio tracks for the task of recording vocals or guitars, and a bunch of plug-ins, with the **Library** open. The only two I will use for this chapter at the beginning are the two named **Tracking Vocal** and the piano, so I can select the others and delete them with the **Delete** key on my computer keyboard.

I can change the default tempo by holding down either the down or up arrow, double-clicking the number, and typing in my desired tempo, or rhythmically pressing the **Tap Tempo** button multiple times. I can also change the default key, time signature, input and output devices (audio interface), sample rate, frame rate (for video), and surround format, if I am set up with 5.1 or 7.1. All of these are Project Settings, except for the input and output device choices, which are Preferences.

Let's talk about **sample rates**, because it can be a complicated issue and there are lots of opinions out there, and my opinions are precisely that, my opinions.

This is what is simply factual:

- Most of the recordings you have heard and loved were recorded at 44.1 kHz, and that is the sample rate required for CDs.
- 48 kHz is the sample rate required for DVDs and most video editing programs, such as Final Cut Pro, will want your audio files to be at that sample rate.

- Higher sample rates are more demanding on your CPU, and the files are bigger and therefore take up more space on your hard drive. 88.2 kHz will be twice as big as 44.1 kHz, and 96 kHz will be twice as big as 48 kHz.

- Files at higher sample rates can be down-sampled with little harm. Up-sampling has no sonic benefit, only possible compatibility with project sample rates.

This is a matter of debate:

- Audio recorded at higher sample rates sound better.

Many, perhaps even most, think FX plug-ins sound better because they have less "aliasing" at, for example, 96 kHz than 44.1 kHz, but not everybody agrees. Some folks maintain that they can identify, in a blind listening test, an identical recording done at the higher and the lower sample rates and that they prefer one or the other. Everybody concedes that it is a trade-off because of the demands on your computer.

Personally, I am not sure. If I am recording a very important project with first-rate microphones, and mic pres, maybe I go with 96 kHz. Most of the time, I use 48 kHz, because I compose music to picture a lot and it is the most utilized sample rate in the video world. If you don't, 44.1 kHz is just fine.

Now that I have loaded the Songwriter template, I can see that it includes Logic's Drummer with an auto-created Drummer region and three Audio channel strips set up with plug-ins for acoustic guitar, a vocal, a bass guitar, and a Sampler-sampled piano, which is of course MIDI. Also, there are four reverb instances being bussed to aux tracks. If you don't understand the concepts of auxes and bussing, don't worry, I will explain later in the chapter.

Let's set up some Preferences.

SETTING PREFERENCES

Remember, any changes you make to these are global to Logic Pro X and therefore affect past, present, and future projects.

AUDIO PREFERENCES

Under the Logic Pro X menu, navigate to **Preferences | Audio | Devices**. If you have not already selected an audio interface, as we did when opening the template, this is where you will assign it. **Core Audio** should be checked, and if you make any changes in this tab, you need to click the **Apply** button to apply the changes:

Figure 3.3 – Enabling a Core Audio Device in the Audio Preferences

The **I/O Buffer Size** (In/Out) has a range of choices, from a low of 32 to a high of 1024. The lower the size you choose, the lower the latency. Latency is the amount of delay you hear when playing a software instrument or recording an audio part through plug-ins. So why not just choose the lowest number, 32, because who wants more latency?

The answer is that the lower the buffer size the harder your computer has to work, and some audio interfaces have their own drivers rather than just core audio that can be more or less efficient than others. The power of your computer and the efficiency of your audio device's driver will determine how low a buffer setting you can get away with without getting error messages or hearing pops and clicks. If you have a computer that's new enough to run Logic Pro X 10.5 and the necessary macOS, unless you are using very resource-demanding third-party orchestral libraries, you probably will find 128 a nice compromise to start with. All the other settings you can leave set to the defaults.

RECORDING PREFERENCES

By default, Logic records audio as Apple's AIFF format, but there are two other choices, Wave (originally a PC format) and CAF.

Unless you are recording exceptionally long times, such as a half day or more, you can rule out CAF because it is not universally supported. So, now we have **AIFF** and **Wave (BWF)**. Which sounds better?

They sound the same! I recommend that Apple's default notwithstanding, you go with Wave, because it has become an industry standard.

While there is controversy about sample rates, there is none about 16 versus 24 bit rates. A higher bit rate allows you to record at a lower signal and raise the gain later because of all the thousands of extra bits. Yes, the audio files are larger, but hard drives are cheap now. You want **24-Bit Recording** checked.

Below that, you can see the choices of how overlapping track recordings are handled:

Figure 3.4 – Recording Preferences

While if I am creating a pop song, I may want different behavior than if I am doing an orchestral piece for film/TV, for now, leave these with the default.

Two Preferences that I recommend you disable are in the **Audio** tab. Although they are designed to be helpful with the **Input** button, which is represented by the letter I you see on the Track Reader, experience has led me to conclude that they cause confusion more than they help:

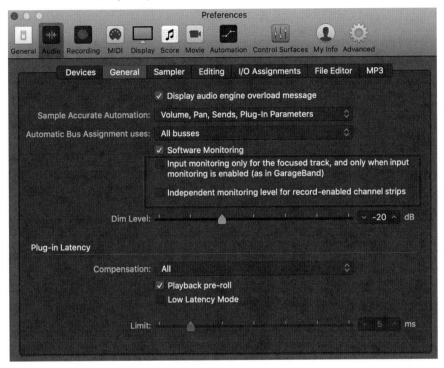

Figure 3.5 – Recording Preferences I recommend you uncheck

DISPLAY PREFERENCES

Moving on to these, you may find you don't need to change a thing in the **General** tab, but I have a high-resolution second display and my eyesight is not so great, so I find checking the **Large local windows**, **Large Inspectors**, **Wide playhead**, and **Show default** values all helpful.

> NOTE
> If you change the language, you will need to quit Logic and restart it.

As I explained earlier in the book, Preferences are global to Logic Pro X. Any changes you make affect past, present, and future projects.

PROJECT SETTINGS

Under the **File** menu, navigate to **Project Settings | General**.

There is a new project setting for dynamic loading of plugins as you need them, which you may find helpful for large projects, and it is on by default. If you don't want this, go to **General | Opening Project | Only load plug-ins needed for project playback**, and uncheck it. Unless you save it as a template though, you will have to keep doing this, which, frankly, I wish were not the case.

For now, we can leave the Project Settings. Because I am just going to record a vocal and a MIDI piano part, I will delete the other tracks from my Track List.

SETTING LEVELS

I am going to get a bit geeky here for a minute and talk about how Logic handles incoming signals. Logic has a *floating point* architecture, which means it adjusts its headroom automatically to incoming signal, so that any channel strip can go into the red without creating digital distortion, **except the Stereo Output**.

When you are setting your levels to record audio, if it is going into the red you are recording it at a distorted level, and that is not good. In the analog world, we generally tried to record as "hot" as possible so as to eliminate the inherent noise, but with digital 24-bit recording it is not necessary to do this. As long as the level is even a little way into the meter reading, it is OK.

I will be singing into a microphone to demonstrate. On your **Input** on the **Audio** channel strip, you must make sure it is set to the correct input of your audio interface that your microphone (or instrument) is plugged in to. In my example, it is **Input 1**:

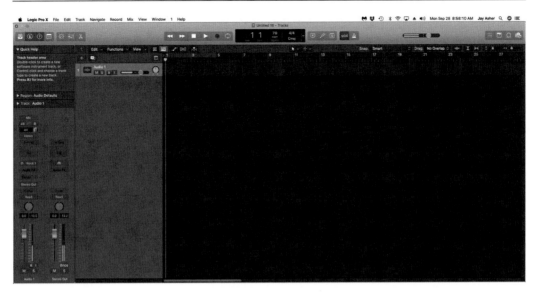

Figure 3.6 – An armed Audio Track with Input 1 receiving level

> **NOTE**
>
> If you see **Input 1-2** to the left of the **Input** assignment field, that means you have a stereo channel strip, indicated by two circles, unlike the one you see in my picture. Simply click on it and it turns to mono.

How you set the incoming levels will depend on the audio interface you own. Most have physical gain knobs that you turn, like the Focusrite Scarlett series. Some have a software control panel and/or knobs to adjust the gain. If you own an Apogee audio interface, as I do, you can set the incoming level directly on the Audio channel strip's Audio Device Controls.

Whatever level you set the gain at, if your signal is registering on the channel strip, even in the lower third, you are fine.

You can, of course, set it higher if you like, as long as you don't see the red clip light come on.

I am ready to record a short vocal for *Mary Had A Little Lamb* to a simple piano accompaniment I have played in. Hooray!

> NOTE
>
> You will want to record listening through headphones with your speakers off so that you don't get feedback or record the sound of the other tracks playing through the speakers.

On the Audio channel strip, I see a number of FX plug-ins that change the sound. You needn't worry that they will be recorded as part of the performance. You are only monitoring through them and can change their settings, delete them, and replace them to your heart's content. To turn them off, simply drag the mouse or trackpad over the left side of them where you will see power buttons. As you do so, they will then be grayed out, as the DeEsser 2 and Echo FX are in this picture, and bypassed so you do not hear them:

Figure 3.7 – Bypassed plug-ins

> NOTE
>
> If I want to create a second audio track for doubling or harmony, I can, either by clicking the + at the top of the track list or by navigating to the **Track** menu and choosing **New Tracks**.

You may or may not want to record listening to a click, played by Logic's metronome.

Go to **Project Settings | Metronome** or hold the mouse or trackpad down on the metronome icon for your choices.

In the nearby Recording Project Settings, you can choose how many bars you want for a Count-in. Since my song begins with a three-beat piano introduction, I don't need a count-in.

> NOTE
>
> From now on, when I describe performing an action using a mouse, know that on a laptop it will be a trackpad.

RECORDING WITH A CYCLE

Cycle recording is recording the same bars over and over without pausing in between attempts. Logic gives you several options for a cycle recording workflow.

CYCLE RECORDING WITH TAKE FOLDERS

Take Folders was the default choice for overlapping recordings in Cycle mode in our Recording Preferences, so there's nothing I need to change now. To set the cycle, I select my piano region and press **U** and I am ready to go.

I am going to sing *Mary Had A Little Lamb* three times without stopping, each time a bit differently. I make sure that the track is armed by clicking the **R** button on the track header or at the bottom of the channel strip in the Inspector (the flashing **R** in the track header) and I either press the **Record** button in the transport or press *R* on my keyboard, and away I go! If you have downloaded the `Chapter 3.logicx` project, you can see and hear what I have described.

What I have now created is called a **Take Folder**. I will be able to use any one of them or drag over sections of each to make a comp, which is how musicians and engineers have always referred to a composite. You see the three takes and at the top of the Take Folder, the composite. In this picture, it entirely comprises take 1; the other two takes are muted, and the comp is named **Comp A**:

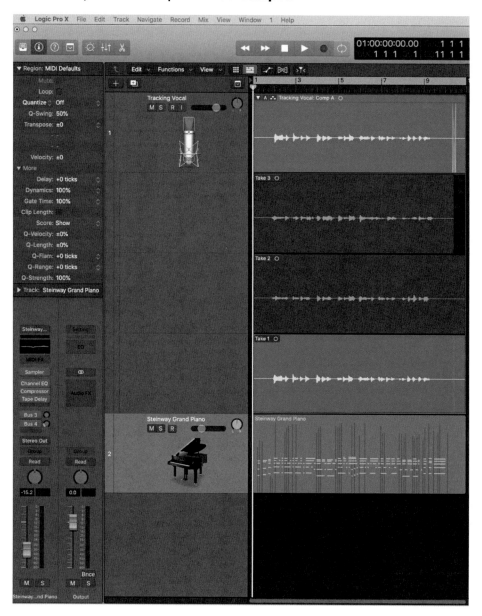

Figure 3.8 – A Take Folder

The next steps I am going to perform could just as easily be in the next chapter on audio editing, but I think it makes sense to do it now. To make it easier to distinguish between the takes, I am going to give each the gift of color.

> NOTE
> There is an auto-colorize option in the **Recording** tab of the **Project Settings**, but for this purpose I recommend you take matters into your own hands.

Pressing **Option + C** on your computer keyboard opens the color palette:

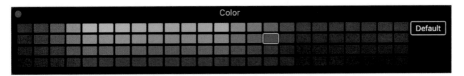

Figure 3.9 – The Color Palette

I select each take and give it a different color, then zoom in by selecting the regions and pressing **Z**. Alternatively, I can hold the **Command** key and press the right arrow and the down arrow for the view I want.

I decide to select the first half of take 1 and the second half of take 2 with a method called **Quick Swipe Comping**.

QUICK SWIPE COMPING

With take 1 selected, I position my Pointer tool over the middle of take 2 and simply drag it to the right. Fantastic, smooth as a baby's bottom, and Logic even creates a crossfade where I switched takes so that there is no audible click. This is a definite candidate for my final choice, but I may want to try other comps.

Comp A is not very descriptive, is it? Holding the mouse down on the **A** at the top left of the **Take Folder** or pressing **Shift + T** allows me to rename it. I rename it *pretty darned good*.

Time to try another one. Although you don't have to, I recommend holding the mouse down on the **A** in the **Take Folder** header and duplicating the comp. I just find it quicker and easier.

I now have Comp B to manipulate. This time, I begin with take 2 and then switch to take 1. Again, not bad, so I rename it *Also doesn't suck*.

I can go on creating more if I want to, but I am pretty happy with my choices. I can leave it in this state, or I can flatten it by pressing down on the **A** and choosing that or using the key command, which will lay the regions out with the crossfades on the track, eliminating the **take folder**. This gives me the ability later on to edit the regions, including the crossfades. I can also do Flatten and Merge, which will create a new audio file, incorporating the crossfades, eliminating the **Take Folder** as well while still leaving the original audio file, consisting of the three take regions, intact on my drive.

I am by nature a cautious man, so before I decide what to do next, I want to always be able to return to my project at this stage of its development. The answer to this is to create a **Project Alternative**.

PROJECT ALTERNATIVES

Under the **File** menu, navigate to **Project Alternatives** | **New Alternative**. A dialog box appears to give you the chance to name it. For now, I will leave it as its default name. I suggest you perhaps name it by date and time.

I decide to flatten and merge the take folder and save the project. I am now free to continue, secure in the knowledge that if anything goes awry, I can always return to its previous state by again going to the **File** menu to **Project Alternatives** and simply choosing the original version.

REGION GAIN

Remember that I told you that with 24-bit recording, you did not have to record hot? Well, sure enough, my recording is not very loud and, looking at the waveform, I see that it isn't that big.

No worries, because if I select the region and look in the Region inspector, there is a **Gain** field that I can either drag up or type in a decibel amount and it will be louder, and the waveform will be bigger.

OTHER CYCLE AUDIO RECORDING OPTIONS

Take Folders are the most user-friendly method for people new to audio recording, but there are other options.

If in **Recording Preferences** | **Audio** you change the choice to **Create Tracks and Mute**, it behaves similarly but creates new tracks flowing through the same Audio channel strip, muting the previous one so that while you are recording, you don't hear the previous passes. (You can later select them and pack them into a take folder, but if you want to end up with a take folder, why not just use that preference?)

Another choice is **Create Track Alternatives**, but I am going to wait until we get to recording MIDI in *Chapter 5, Recording MIDI,* to demonstrate this choice because I find it more useful for MIDI than audio.

RECORDING WITHOUT A CYCLE

All three options, **Create Take Folder**, **Create New Track**, and **Create Track Alternative**, are the same as with cycle recording, but you stop in between takes.

Let's say that you are now pretty happy with your audio recording, whichever method you used, but there is a specific section you are not happy with that you would like to replace and have Logic help you with it automatically. For this task, Autopunch is your friend.

Return to **Customize Control and Display** and under **Modes and Functions**, check both **Autopunch** and **Replace**. You will now see two buttons to the right of the LCD. The X toggles Replace on and off and the up and down arrows toggle Autopunch:

Figure 3.10 – Autopunch and Replace buttons in the control bar

Now you will understand one of the reasons I recommended in the previous chapter enabling **Sample Rate** or **Punch Locators** in the LCD. You can see the red bar that shows in the punch locators, and you can either drag it to the section you want and adjust the length or double-click on the numbers and type in your locators.

You can now record and Logic will Autopunch your new audio recording within the locators. (If you like, you can turn on Cycle, but unfortunately it will only Autopunch during the first pass of the Cycle.):

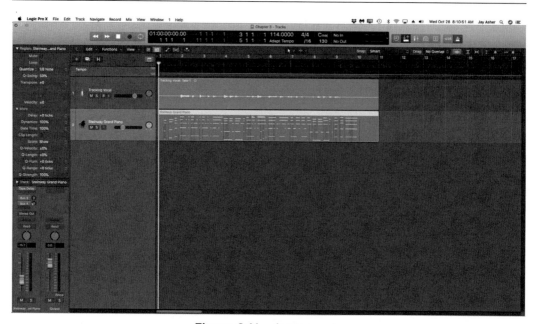

Figure 3.11 – Autopunch

Uh-oh, what if I am not happy with that punch? Did I ruin my original recording? No! This is a non-destructive process. Press **Command + Z** to undo, and you are back to where you were.

TAPE RECORDER STYLE PUNCHING IN/OUT

Many of us who come from the world of tape recorders still like recording along and simply punching in and punching out when we deem it necessary, without stopping. In Logic Pro X, we do this with **Quick Punch** and using **Record Toggle**.

Hold the mouse down on the **Record** button, check **Allow Quick Punch-in,** and switch to **Record/Record Toggle**. Or, with **Quick Punch-in** enabled, instead of pressing **R** to go in and out of record, press the asterisk key. This method is still especially helpful when you are running Logic but someone else is performing.

RECORDING WITHOUT A CLICK WITH SMART TEMPO

While it certainly is possible to record to a click without the result sounding mechanical, it is freeing to record without one. Musicians refer to this technique as Rubato, the traditional Italian name.

You can record both audio and MIDI with software instruments freely, but let's try it here with audio with a Logic Pro X feature that I believe is simply amazing:

1. Set your project tempo to approximately what you want it to be.

2. In the Control bar's LCD, change the setting from **Keep Tempo** to **Adapt Tempo**.

3. Record!

I recorded the first phrase of the *Battle Hymn of the Republic* because it's public domain and has strong downbeats, which really helps Smart Tempo's analysis. Here, you can see the result:

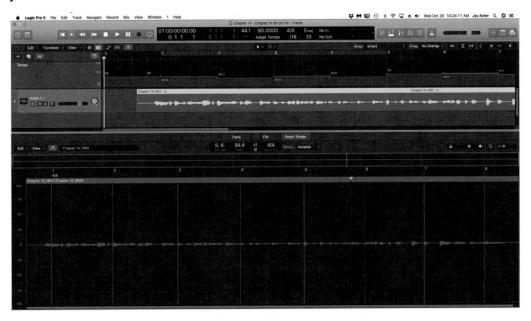

Figure 3.12 – A Rubato vocal recording

Smart Tempo has correctly analyzed the tempo I sang and created a tempo map. Now I can play subsequent parts and hear the tempo so that they will work together. Amazing!

As we have learned, Project Settings are not global, so we may now want to save this project as a template to begin with in the future.

SAVING A TEMPLATE

To save a template, follow these steps:

1. Save your project.
2. Press **Command** + **A** to select all the regions and delete them.
3. Press **F** to open the browser and in the **Project** tab, select all the audio regions and delete them. This will **not** delete them from your drive.
4. Under the **File** menu, choose **Save as Template** and name it.
5. Close the project without saving it again so that the project will remember the audio files' locations that are in the project.

The next time you open Logic Pro X, you will see a folder named **My Templates**, and there it will be.

SUMMARY

You have now been introduced to Logic Pro X's included Project Templates, with some recommendations for your Preferences. As you discovered, there are also Project Settings for you to choose from that will affect how you record audio. Setting levels properly is important. Finally, you can record with or without cycling with different workflows, as explained, and fix takes with Autopunch and old-fashioned tape-recorder-style punch in/out. When you have Project Settings and track choices that you like, you may well want to save them as a template.

In the next chapter, we will explore the options for soloing and muting tracks and regions, as well as renaming them. We will learn how to copy and repeat regions, and the effect the Snap and Drag settings have on the behavior. We will also learn about the Audio Track Editor and Audio File Editor, how they differ, and where they are useful.

4 EDITING AUDIO

Logic Pro X makes editing audio easy with its tools to copy sections, delete sections, and replace sections, all non-destructively in the **Tracks area**. There are also two other places to edit audio, the **Track Editor** and the **File Editor**. The former is also non-destructive while the latter is destructive.

Specifically, this chapter covers the following topics:

- Soloing and muting in Logic Pro X
- Renaming and colorizing tracks and regions
- Zooming in and out on regions
- Copying and repeating regions using the Snap and Drag settings
- Working with an imported audio file in the Audio Track Editor

Logic Pro X gives you many ways to solo and mute either tracks or regions, and it can get confusing. Let's try to give you some clarity on this first.

SOLOING AND MUTING TRACKS AND REGIONS

Frequently, you will want and need to solo or mute tracks and regions while editing audio, and frankly, it can be confusing in Logic, because there are so many ways.

Here you see the beginnings of a little blues song I created for this chapter:

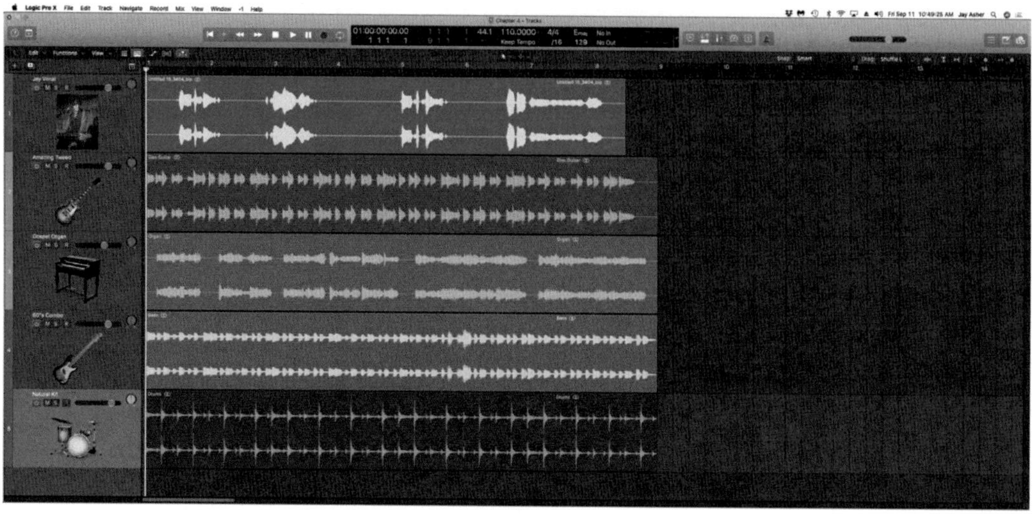

Figure 4.1 – My blues song tracks and regions

MUTE/SOLO BUTTONS ON THE TRACK HEADER

On my track header in the preceding screenshot, you can see an **M** and an **S**, for mute and solo. If you don't see it, you need to configure the track header, and this is something you will need to know how to do, so let's take advantage of this opportunity to learn how.

If you right-click (or **Ctrl**-click) in the track header, or simply press **Option + T**, it brings up a window in which you can choose the things you want to see in the track header, including the **Mute** and **Solo** buttons. (If, like me, you find that you frequently have multiple tracks flowing through a channel strip, I recommend you also add the **Power On/Off** button. Since the **Mute/Solo** buttons affect the channel strip, not the individual track, you need the **Power** button to solo or mute tracks discretely.)

Once you have made your choices, navigate to the gear icon at the bottom of the panel, as shown in the following screenshot, and select **Store as User Defaults**:

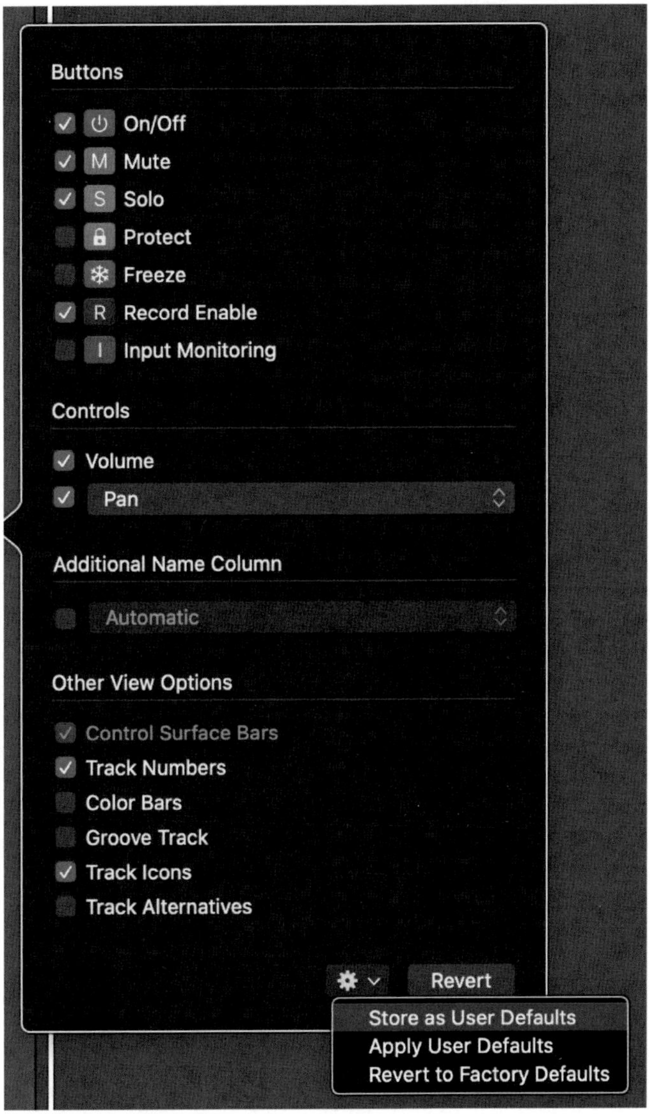

Buttons

- ☑ ⏻ On/Off
- ☑ M Mute
- ☑ S Solo
- ☐ 🔒 Protect
- ☐ ❄ Freeze
- ☑ R Record Enable
- ☐ I Input Monitoring

Controls

- ☑ Volume
- ☑ Pan ↕

Additional Name Column

- ☐ Automatic ↕

Other View Options

- ☑ Control Surface Bars
- ☑ Track Numbers
- ☐ Color Bars
- ☐ Groove Track
- ☑ Track Icons
- ☐ Track Alternatives

⚙ ∨ | Revert

Store as User Defaults
Apply User Defaults
Revert to Factory Defaults

Figure 4.2 – Storing Track Header defaults

The most direct way to solo a channel strip is to simply press the **S** button in the Track Header or press **S** on your computer keyboard. When you do so, the **S** button turns yellow. A yellow **S** button also appears at the top of the Track List, and the **M** button on all the other channel strips turn to a blinking blue.

If you **Shift**-click the Track Headers, then the **S** button at the top of the Track List toggles that selection on and off.

Well, that's fine, but there is one drawback to this method. If I select a different Track Header, it doesn't change to soloing that selection. There are times when that may well be how I want it to behave, but for me personally, those occasions are very rare.

MUTE/SOLO BUTTONS ON THE CHANNEL STRIP IN THE MIXER

Press **X** to open the Mixer and on the channel strip faders, you will see the same **S** and **M** buttons as on the Track Header, and they behave identically to the way they do on the Track Header.

REGION SOLO BUTTON IN THE CONTROL BAR

This is the method of soloing I employ most frequently:

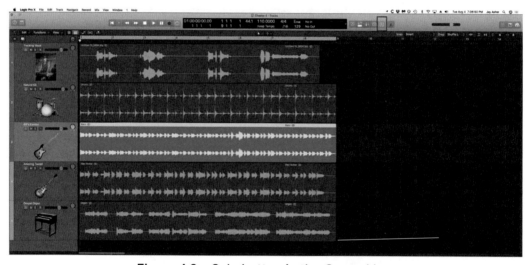

Figure 4.3 – Solo button in the Control bar

With the **S** in the Control bar checked, you will notice that it does update when you select a different Track Header, as by default, selecting the Track Header selects the regions on that track. This is especially helpful when playing back your project and listening for various things. Pressing **Ctrl + S** *also* toggles this region solo button on and off. If in your **Preferences | General | Editing** tab you have unchecked **select tracks on region/marquee** selection, then with solo switched on in the Control bar, selecting regions will not select the tracks. Then, it will only solo the one or more regions you select in the Tracks area.

> NOTE
> I recommend that you do uncheck it, because in my opinion, unlike selecting regions when you click on a Track Header, which is helpful, I think this option creates more problems than it solves.

Another option is to change one of your tools to the Solo tool. With the Solo tool, you can solo regions by holding down the Solo tool on them. It does take a second or two to kick in though, when you choose a different region during playback.

RENAMING AND COLORIZING TRACKS AND REGIONS

Before you get down to some serious audio editing, you may want to rename your tracks and regions so that they are consistent.

You can rename a region either by changing your left-click tool from the Pointer to the Text tool. With the Text tool, you can then simply select the name on the region and type in the new name. Even easier, after selecting the region with the Pointer tool, just press **Shift + N**.

Alternatively, with the region selected, you can click on the name in the Region Inspector and do it there.

In the following screenshot, you see that my track names and region names are not consistent with each other, nor are their colors:

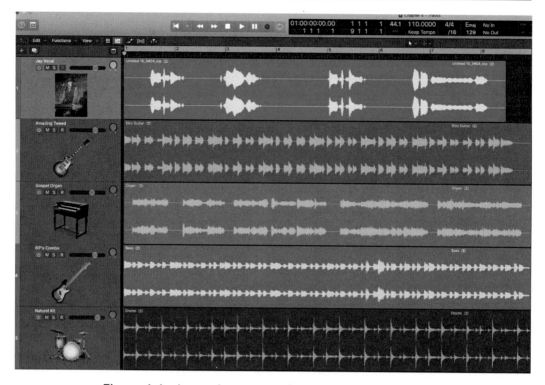

Figure 4.4 – Inconsistent track/region names and colors

On track 1, I want the region to have the track name, while on the other tracks I want each track to have the region name and I want the region's colors to be the track's colors.

Easy-peasy.

With track 1 selected, go under the **Functions** menu and find **Name Regions/Cells by Track Name**, which has the default key command of **Option + Shift + N**.

Select the other four regions and under the **Functions** menu, find **Name Track by Region/Cell Name**, which has the default key command of **Option + Shift + Command + N**.

Then, find **Color Track by Region/Cell Name**, which has the default key command of **Option + Shift + Command + C**.

Now, we are ready to start editing.

ZOOMING IN AND OUT ON REGIONS

When you are editing, especially with audio waveforms, you will want to zoom in and out to accommodate the regions or sections of regions you are trying to edit.

Logic, being Logic, gives you a number of ways to do this.

Let's practice zooming in on some regions. Press **2** to open Screenset 2, as shown in the following screenshot. (We will discuss the use of screensets more deeply in *Chapter 13, Organizing for the Mix*):

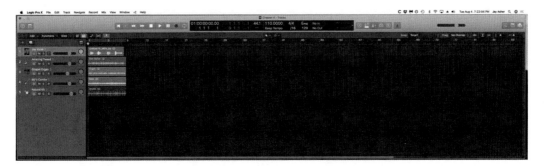

Figure 4.5 – Regions for zooming

In the upper-right corner of the **Tracks** area are two zoom sliders: vertical and horizontal, highlighted on the right of the following screenshot:

Figure 4.6 – Zoom sliders

Dragging these sliders zooms in or out of all the regions.

There are also a bunch of helpful key commands already assigned:

1. Press **Option + K** to open the **Key Commands** window.

2. In the search field, type the word `zoom`:

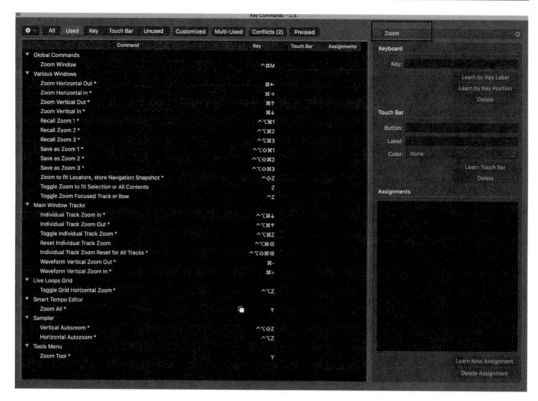

Figure 4.7 – Preassigned zoom key commands

3. Select the **Used** button.

Wow, that is a lot of options! The one I rely on most is **Toggle Zoom to fit Selection or All Content**. No matter the number of regions you select, your selection fills the window by simply pressing **Z**, and pressing **Z** again returns it to its original zoom level.

COPYING AND REPEATING REGIONS

Presently, my song is only 8 bars long and I want to make it longer. Logic being Logic, there are a few user-friendly ways.

COPYING BY HOLDING OPTION + DRAGGING

I decide to mute my vocals and work on the instrument tracks. I can copy the regions easily by holding the **Option** key and dragging them, keeping an eye on the help tag for positioning.

NOTE

If when you do this, but you do not first release the mouse and *then* the **Option** key, you will find that instead of copying it, you have moved it.

COPYING PARTS OF REGIONS WITH THE MARQUEE TOOL

My chord progression is a basic blues phrase: G7 for 2 bars, C7 for 2 bars, G7 for 2 bars, D7 for two bars. Now, I want the next section to be: C7 for 1 bar, D7 for 1bar, C7 for 1 bar, D7 for 1 bar C7 for 3 bars, and finally, D7 for 1 bar.

The Marquee tool is ideal for this task, but my **Snap settings** can make it even easier.

If you hold down the mouse on the field to the right of **Snap**, you'll see that you have the following settings options:

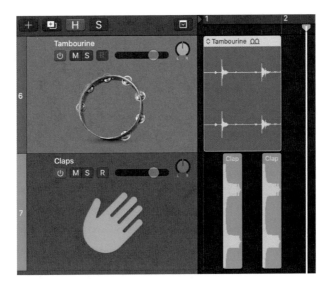

Figure 4.8 – Snap settings

Smart means Logic takes into account how zoomed in you are on the Tracks area and frequently makes the right decisions, but precision and ease of use is key for me here, as I want to copy a section of the guitar, bass, and organ that begins exactly on bar 3 and copy them exactly to bar 17. So, it makes sense to change from **Smart**

to **Bar**. If it began a bit earlier or later than precisely bar 3, **Snap Regions to Relative Value** would be the right choice, but here I want **Absolute Value**.

By default, the **Command**-click tool is set to the Marquee tool.

1. While holding the **Command** key, I drag over the guitar, bass, organ, and drums from bar 3 to bar 4, and if I hit play, I hear that measure.

2. If I click on the selection with the Pointer tool, it creates new regions that I can copy, which works fine, but I don't have to.

3. Instead, I simply **Option**-drag them to bar 17.

4. Since I want them to be a D7, with the new guitar, bass, and organ regions selected, in the Region Inspector I enter +2 next to **Transpose**. (Obviously, I don't want to transpose the drums.)

5. I select 6 new regions and copy them to bar 19, then bar 21.

6. I select the regions at bar 17 and copy them to bar 23, then 24, then 25.

7. Bar 8 is perfect to finish this section. I select the regions and copy them to bar 24 with the Marquee tool.

Almost perfect!

EDITING WITH SHUFFLE MODE

We now have seen the power of changing the Snap settings, but the Drag settings have a powerful effect as well.

I think this section might be more powerful without the section you see highlighted in this screenshot, going instead to the end of the regions:

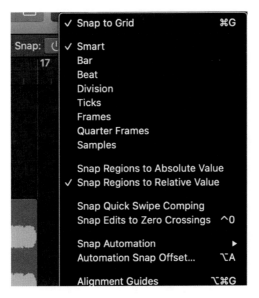

Figure 4.9 – Sections of regions selected with the Marquee tool

To ensure this works seamlessly, I want to change the **Drag** from **No Overlap** to **Shuffle L** (left).

Now when I delete the Marquee tool selections, the following material snaps right to the border of the previous sections of the region.

Fantastic!

REPEAT REGIONS

In the **Tracks area** local menu called **Edit**, you can scroll down to **Repeat**, and see that you have the option to **repeat selected regions/cells/events** once or multiple times. Only the former is assigned to a key command, which I think is a mistake. If you choose **Multiple**, by default it comes up as **1**, but also gives you other options, as you see here:

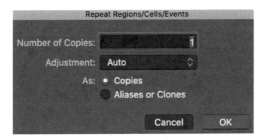

Figure 4.10 – Repeat Multiple options

The advantage of choosing **Copies** is that you can have independent control of each region, knowing that the changes you make to one region will not affect the others. There may be times, however, when you want any edit you do to one region to affect all the others. That is where **Aliases** or **Clones** should be your choice.

LOOPING REGIONS

Looping regions is a quick and easy way to repeat regions. But in this example, taken from another project, we can see an example where we have a region length inconsistency that we need to deal with first:

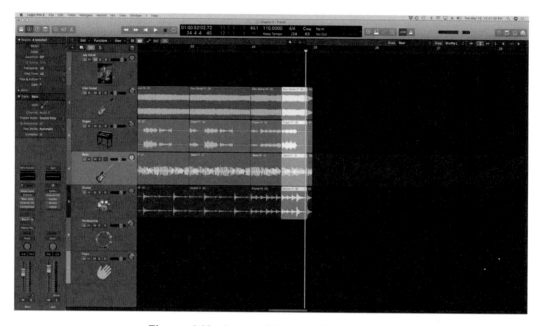

Figure 4.11 – Inconsistent region lengths

The **Tambourine** region is exactly one measure long and will loop perfectly. With it selected, I can either press **L** to loop it, check the **Loop** box in the **Region Inspector**, or position the Pointer tool in the upper-right corner and it changes to the Loop tool, allowing me to draw in the number of times I want it to loop.

But looping the claps on beats 2 and 4 is a problem. **Region folders** to the rescue!

Under the **Functions** menu, we need to navigate to **Folder | Pack Folder**, and my claps are now in a one-bar folder that loops perfectly.

WORKING WITH AN IMPORTED AUDIO FILE IN THE AUDIO TRACK EDITOR

Returning to our `Chapter 4.logicx` project, let's learn a couple of ways to import an audio file into a Logic project.

You can open the **All Files Browser** by clicking the icon in the Control bar, or pressing **F**, and then navigating to where the file is stored:

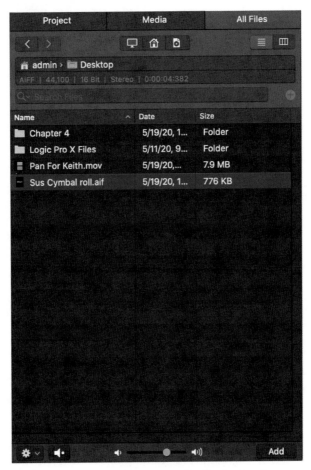

Figure 4.12 – Selecting an audio file in the Browser

The advantage of importing an audio file this way is that you can click the speaker icon at the bottom of the window to audition it.

To add an audio file into the Tracks area at a specific position in the project, change the left-click or **Command**-click default tool to the Pencil tool, then hold it down on the track in the Tracks area at that position.

Alternatively, you can import an audio file by dragging it from the Finder to the same place or go to the **File** menu | **Import** | **Audio File**.

AUDIO TRACK EDITOR

Once it is in your project and you have placed it approximately where you want it to go, you can of course move it around in the timeline to get it exactly where you want it, but the Audio Track Editor is more efficient for doing so.

With the region selected, press **E** and make sure you are in the Track view. As with the Tracks area, anything you do here is non-destructive:

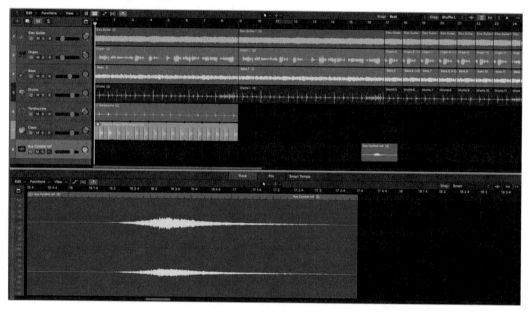

Figure 4.13 – An imported audio file in the Audio Track Editor

I want to position the region so that the loudest part lands right in bar 17. In the Audio Track Editor, it's nice and large, especially if I enable the waveform zoom by pressing the icon to the right of the **Snap** menu.

Now, it's super easy to drag it so that it crests at bar 17.

For my ears, though, it takes a little long to happen. If I position the Pointer on the lower-left corner, the Pointer tool changes to the Resize tool and I can drag it to the right to shorten it. I can then do the same thing on the right side, so it now unfolds and exits more quickly. But it isn't as smooth as I might like, so I need to add some fades.

While I can change one of my tools to the Fade tool, holding **Shift + Control** in the Audio Track Editor changes the Pointer tool to the Fade tool while I hold the keys down, and I can then draw in fades and then tweak them by again holding down that key combination and adjusting the fade.

I ended up with this; it sounds really good and peaks where I want it to peak:

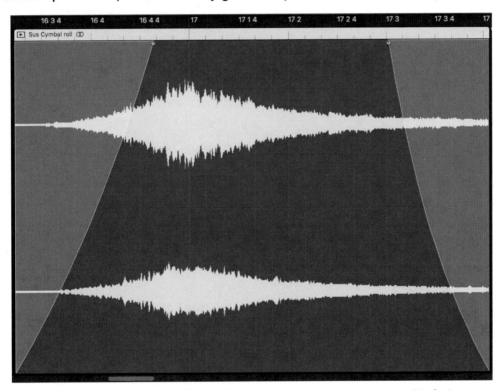

Figure 4.14 – The audio file well positioned, shortened, and with fades

AUDIO FILE EDITOR

This is the editor where you do destructive audio editing. A few years ago, even though this book is for beginners, I would have felt the need to introduce you to some things to do with it, but frankly, it is rarely necessary to do destructive audio editing in Logic Pro X anymore, so I will only show you a screenshot of some of its functions and caution you to work from a copy of the original audio file in this editor so that you don't risk damaging your original audio file:

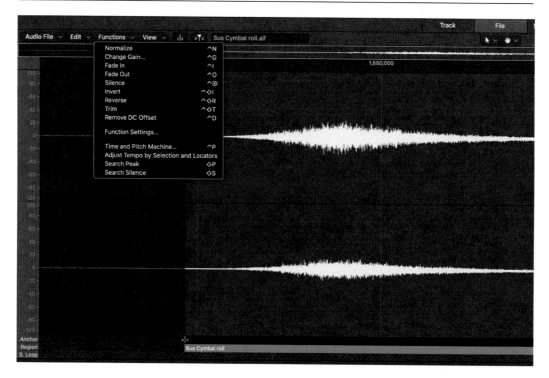

Figure 4.15 – Audio File Editor

SUMMARY

In this chapter, we covered different ways of soloing and muting tracks and regions. You have learned how to use the Marquee tool to copy, repeat, and move regions and parts of regions in the Tracks area, and how the Snap settings and modes affect the result. Also, you are now familiar with techniques for importing audio files and working with them in the Audio Track Editor, while the destructive Audio File Editor was briefly discussed.

In the next chapter, we will become familiar with how to record freely, without a click. You will learn a way to change the project's tempo with an imported audio file, along with the Flex Time and Flex Pitch tools, which are great tools for improving the timing and tuning of your audio recordings. Finally, we will explore the history of Varispeed, and use Logic's version to speed up or slow down an entire project without changing pitch, unless we want to.

5 RECORDING MIDI

As previously explained in *Chapter 1, Beginning with Logic Pro X 10.5*, MIDI is simply a set of instructions that can be utilized by a keyboard, tone module, drum machine, or Software Instrument that is capable of understanding the messages and responding to them.

We will be focusing on **Software Instruments**, and Logic Pro X comes with a great array of them.

This chapter will cover the following main topics:

- Recording MIDI parts with Logic Pro X's many Software Instruments
- Logic's MIDI editors
- Correcting timing with quantization
- Creating interesting layered sounds with Summing Stacks
- Making one track follow the feel of another

LOGIC PRO X'S SOFTWARE INSTRUMENTS

As you can see in the following screenshot, Logic comes with a dazzling array of Software Instruments. Yes, there are lots of great third-party Software Instruments as well, but I suggest you become conversant with the Logic content before you reach for your wallet:

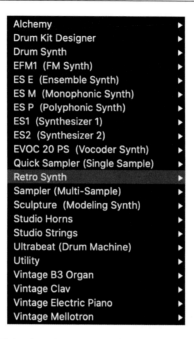

Figure 5.1 – Logic Pro's Software Instruments

LOGIC PRO X'S BUILT-IN HELP

Logic comes with built-in *manuals* that you can access under the **Help** menu. One that you will find very helpful specifically deals with Logic's Software Instruments.

> IMPORTANT NOTE
>
> If you would like a downloadable version, you can go to the website and click on the ones that say web link: https://support. apple.com/en-gb/logic-pro.

GARAGEBAND VERSUS LOGIC PRO INSTRUMENTS

Follow these steps to get started with Logic Pro instruments:

1. Open a new Logic empty project and create an empty Software Instrument track.

2. Press **O** to open the **Loop Browser** and drag any **Green Apple Loop** into the workspace. I have chosen **12 String Dream 02**.

3. With the region selected, press **U** to create a Cycle and play it.

You will see in the Inspector that Logic has loaded a Software Instrument named **Guitar** with three FX plugins. When you look at the picture of the Software Instruments, you do not see *guitar*.

Guitar is actually a simplified version of Logic's sampler that comes with GarageBand. If you click on it to open it, you will see this **Graphical User Interface (GUI)**:

Figure 5.2 – A GarageBand sampler instrument

Hold the mouse down on the **Guitar** instrument in the Inspector and scroll to **Sampler** (multi-sample) stereo and now you will see the Logic version:

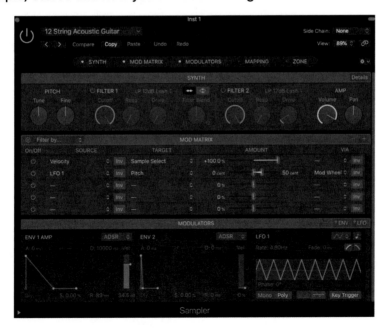

Figure 5.3 – The Logic Pro equivalent of the GarageBand sampler instrument

Of course, the question is, does it sound different? Maybe *a little*, because the Logic version has more filters, but not like night and day.

Next, let's take a look at the MIDI editors.

VIEWING A MIDI REGION IN THE LOGIC PRO MIDI EDITORS

With the region selected, press **P** to open **Piano Roll**. The **Piano Roll** editor is by far the most utilized editor among Logic users. Here, you will see the MIDI notes' positions, pitches, lengths, and velocity, indicated by color. The bluer it is, the softer the velocity; the more reddish, the louder the velocity. All of this is, of course, editable, which we will do in the next chapter.

Now, press **N** to open the **Score Editor**, where you will see the notes as musical notation. It's a very deep editor because it allows you to make the MIDI sound one way while appearing as another, and you can print out parts and entire scores. It is so deep that I wrote an entire book on it. We won't be spending much time on it in this book for that reason.

> NOTE
> Notice that when I open the **Score Editor**, **Piano Roll** disappears, and vice versa. Under the **Window** menu are standalone windows for each that you can open so that you can see them both, screen real estate permitting.

If you press **D**, you open the **List** editors. The **Event List** editor is the one we want to explore:

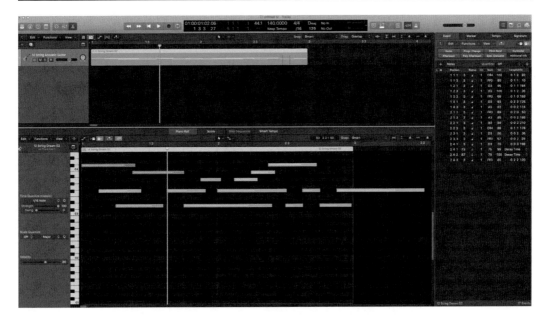

Figure 5.4 – The List editors in Logic Pro

This is perhaps the most over-looked MIDI editor, and for me, it is essential to my workflow. Because it is a List editor, as you can see, I can have both **Piano Roll** and the **Event List** open.

So, what are we seeing here? At the top are buttons to filter in/out different kinds of MIDI events. If you click on **Notes**, it grays out, and now the **Event List** is empty because, in this Apple Loop, the only included MIDI events are notes.

The first column is **Position**. This tells you where in the project the event occurs. The first note is at **1 1 1 3**. What does that mean?

The first number is the bar; the second number is the beat, which is a quarter note in 4/4 time; the third number in the sixteenth note within the beat; and the last number is the tick. A tick is the smallest unit of timing resolution in a MIDI sequencer. Logic has 240 ticks per sixteenth note, so the three you see here are, therefore, just a teensy bit of the very beginning of the project.

The next column is called **Status**, and we see a *Note* symbol on each. As you will see later in the chapter, not all MIDI events will have that symbol.

Ch is short for MIDI channel. With hardware synths and samplers, this can choose specific sounds, but with Logic, it mostly has to do with how it appears in the **Score Editor** unless you are working with multi-timbral instruments, which we will not be dealing with in this book.

Clearly, **Num** is a list of the pitches. By default, C3 is middle C in Logic, which is the Yamaha convention. Roland says its C4, which on an 88-note keyboard it is, but more users have smaller keyboards. If you feel the need to change it, you can in **Preferences | Display | General**.

Val is the velocity of the note. In MIDI, all measurements can range from 1 to 127.

Length is just that, the length of the note, and the numbers work the same way as they do with **Position**.

MIDI CONTINUOUS CONTROLLERS

There are 127 MIDI **Continous Controllers** (**CCs**, as they are commonly known). The ones most often employed are CC1-Modwheel, CC7-MIDI volume, CC11-Expression, and CC 64-Sustain. With third-party Software Instrument libraries, how they control them is all over the map. With Logic Pro, they are more consistent. CC1 will usually control vibrato, CC7 and CC11 will control volume, and CC64 will control sustain. You can generate them from a keyboard controller or device, and you can step enter them.

RECORDING MIDI WITH MERGE

We already visited this window when we set our recording preferences for audio, but since we may want to make different choices when recording MIDI we should return to it now. Go to **Preferences | Recording**. For now, let's have **Merge** as the option for both non-Cycle and Cycle recording.

Merge means that we will add material to existing material when we record again.

Press **Shift + Command + N** to create a new empty project, and create a Software Instrument channel strip with the default patch, which is a **Vintage Electric Piano** (it's a *Fender* Rhodes, but Apple can't tell you that or they would have to pay Fender).

If you have a MIDI keyboard controller connected to your Mac, play it now, and you will hear the sound. As you play, in your control bar, which we customized earlier, you will see the notes or chords as you play them.

If you do not have a physical MIDI keyboard controller connected to your computer, press **Command + K** and the Musical Typing keyboard appears. Notice that you can either play the notes from the virtual keys or from the keys on your computer keyboard.

LET'S GET STARTED!

Make sure that your metronome is set to click while you are recording:

Figure 5.5 – Metronome settings

Play a 4-bar quarter note bass pattern.

> NOTE
>
> If you don't hear the first note, it is because you played it before the beginning of the project at **1111**. In any MIDI editor, simply move it by selecting the note and pressing the semicolon key.

If you don't like it, simply press **Command + Z** to undo it and try again. Now play and record some chords. I am doing eighth notes.

Here is what I came up with:

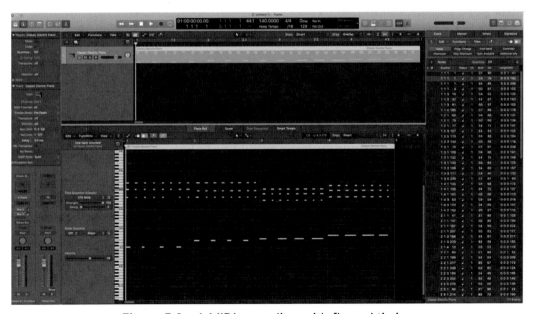

Figure 5.6 – A MIDI recording with flawed timing

Man, I did a lousy job; my timing was terrible! At least I didn't hit any wrong notes. Had I done so, I could simply select the offending notes and hit **Delete**, or if I wanted them but they were on the wrong note, drag them to the correct note in the **Piano Roll** editor.

If you look at either the **Piano Roll** editor or the **Event List**, you can see just how off the grid my timing was. We need to fix this by snapping the notes to the grid. In Logic Pro, we call this **quantizing**. All MIDI quantizing is non-destructive because again, MIDI is just a set of instructions. We will learn how to quantize regions in the next section.

QUANTIZING REGIONS

In the Region inspector, you can quantize as many regions at one time as you like; in this case, just one. I played quarter notes in the bass part and eighth note chords, so my smallest value was an eighth note. I set it to **1/8 Note** and sure enough, it is now smack on the grid. But it sounds like a robot now. This is sometimes referred to as **hard quantizing**.

Am I really stuck with living with bad timing, moving a bunch of notes around in a MIDI editor, or sounding robotic?

No, of course not. We can utilize advanced quantize parameters to achieve a more natural sound.

ADVANCED QUANTIZE PARAMETERS

If you click the **More** disclosure triangle, you will see that more choices become available, including **Q-Flam**, **Q-Range**, and **Q-Strength**. **Q-Flam**, while helpful to add a bit of variance to quantized chords, is not something I find very useful.

But **Q-Strength** certainly is. If I double-click on the field where I see **100 %**, or pull down on it with the mouse, I can set it to a less Draconian value. In this instance, I will try **92 %**.

It is obvious in the editors, especially **Event List**, that it is no longer hard quantized, and when I play it back, it sounds both in time and human.

Q-Range can refine it even more. If I set it to - 8 ticks, I am telling Logic, *if it is 8 or fewer ticks off the grid, leave it alone, but if it is more than that, move it 92% to the grid.*

There is no magic formula for this – it depends on your performance – but skillful use of these settings is the key to getting parts that feel both tight and human.

SETTING A DEFAULT QUANTIZATION SETTING

Personally, I don't care about doing this, but many users do. If you know that in the next part you will be playing eighth notes and you want to default to that quantization, make sure you have no region selected, and in the Region inspector, set it to 1/8 note, and that will be the default.

We have now already recorded MIDI with **Merge** and done some timing correction. Let's learn about some other methods to record MIDI.

OTHER TECHNIQUES FOR RECORDING MIDI

While merging might well be the way you want to record MIDI most often, there are other ways to do it that in specific situations you may prefer:

- Recording MIDI with **Replace**
- Recording MIDI with **Cycle** and **Merge**
- Recording MIDI with **Cycle** and **Create Tracks**
- Recording MIDI with **Cycle** and **Take Folders**

We will also discuss recording MIDI CCs, such as modwheel and expression

RECORDING MIDI WITH REPLACE

Replace means that we will replace material with existing material when we record again.

If in the control bar, click on the **X** button, which turns orange, and now you are in **Replace mode**. But here are a number of ways it can behave, depending on what you choose in **Recording Preferences**:

- **Region Erase**: Erases MIDI regions from the **Tracks** area from the start of the recording until the end of the recording, even if nothing is played.
- **Region Punch**: Erases MIDI regions only where MIDI events have been recorded.
- **Content Erase**: Does not erase MIDI regions but the MIDI content inside of them, from the start of the recording until the end of the recording, even if nothing is played.
- **Content Punch**: Does not erase MIDI regions but the MIDI content inside of them, only where MIDI events have been recorded.

I am mostly a **Region Erase** guy.

I create a new Software Instrument either by clicking the **+** sign at the top of the track list or by doing the following:

1. Open the Library by pressing Y.

2. Navigate to the **Bass** instruments, and load **Fingerstyle Bass**.

3. Then, play a simple bass part. Not bad, but we can do better.

4. Click the **X** button to enable **Replace mode** and play the part again.

Much better this time, and if need be, you can fix notes and quantize accordingly.

RECORDING MIDI WITH CYCLE AND MERGE

This is another option that is good for drum parts, and it mimics old drum machine methodology. It's a very user-friendly way of creating parts with a flow and one you are already familiar with if you have ever played into a drum machine:

1. Create a new Software Instrument and open the Library by pressing **Y**.

2. Navigate to the **Drums** instruments, and load **East Bay**.

3. Set a 4-bar cycle, either by drawing it in the bar ruler or by selecting one of the existing 4-bar regions and pressing **U**.

4. Click the **X** button to disable **Replace mode**.

5. Now play, without stopping, the kick drum, then the snare, then the high hats, and then a tom fill.

In **Piano Roll**, to the right of the **View** menu is the **Collapse** button. By clicking **I**, **Piano Roll** only shows me the notes I played, and it shows me the kit piece names.

Now it just so happens that quantizing to a sixteenth note with some **Q-Strength** works perfectly on the whole region. But I will now show you another way of doing this that gives you more control.

RECORDING MIDI WITH CYCLE AND CREATE TRACKS

Back in **Recording Preferences**, I change the Cycle recording behavior to **Create Tracks**. Now, doing the exact same procedure with the drums, instead of one track I have four tracks flowing through the same channel strip, and each region can be given its own quantization settings.

After, if I want them to be on one track in one region, I can merge them together with the **Glue** tool, or by pressing **Command + J** to merge them.

RECORDING MIDI WITH CYCLE AND CREATE TRACK ALTERNATIVES

Again, back to **Recording Preferences**. This time, I will change the Cycle recording behavior to **Create Track Alternatives**.

By now, you are well familiar with the steps for creating a new Software Instrument and loading a patch from the Library, so I will just tell you that I am using the patch named **Clean Guitar**.

Now, following the exact same procedure as with the drums, I will play three different parts. Next to the name, in the Track Header, I see the letter **C**, with an up and down arrow. This means I have created three track alternatives: **A**, **B**, and **C**.

Holding the mouse down on **C** brings up this menu:

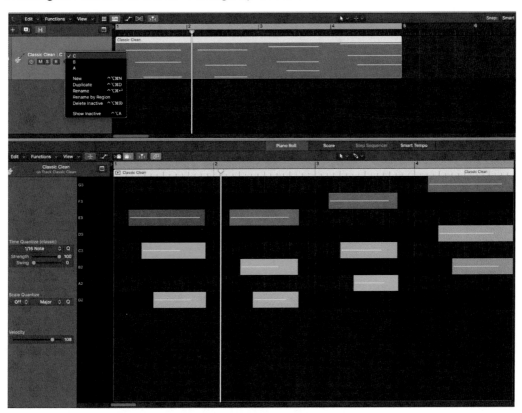

Figure 5.7 – Track alternatives

I can now audition each one to see which one I like best, and when I re-select the region, **Piano Roll** updates to reflect that track alternative.

Selecting **Show Inactive**, or by pressing **Ctrl + option + A**, shows me all three, with two muted, and each has a power button to turn it on instead of the chosen one, and an arrow to move it to the top. I can then either hide or delete the inactive track alternatives.

I love this workflow for MIDI, personally.

Hey, Jay, speaking of audio, what about that nifty **Cycle Recording** with **Take Folders** that we employed to record audio?

RECORDING MIDI WITH CYCLE AND TAKE FOLDERS

Again, back to **Recording Preferences**. This time, I change the Cycle recording behavior to **Change the Preference to this**.

The good news is, you already know how to do this, and it works the same way, except...there is no Quick Swipe Comping the MIDI.

For me, this makes it my least favorite choice. If you disagree, then go back to **Recording Audio** in *Chapter 3, Recording Audio*, and review it.

> NOTE
>
> Remember to keep track of changes to your **Recording Preferences**, because they will affect every project, new, present, or older.

RECORDING MIDI WITH CCS

In addition to playing in notes, you can play in MIDI CCs either at the same time or in additional passes.

Some of what you can do is the following:

- **Record CC 1 - Modwheel**, by manipulating the mod wheel on your keyboard controller, if it has one. Usually, but not always, it will increase/decrease vibrato.

- **Record CC 11 - Expression**, by raising and lowering a connected expression pedal, if you have one plugged in on your keyboard controller. Usually, but not always, it will increase/decrease the volume and sometimes brighten or darken the timbre, but this varies greatly from instrument to instrument.

- **Record CC 64 - Sustain**, by pressing down and releasing a connected sustain (damper) pedal, if you have one plugged in on your keyboard controller. When pressed down, it will sustain the sound when you take your hands off the keys, and end the sound when you release it.

THE ARPEGGIATOR MIDI FX PLUGIN

While an arpeggiator can be used with any Software Instrument, traditionally we think of them as being associated with hardware synthesizers, as almost all of them have one built-in. Well, Logic has a MIDI plugin for this purpose, and it is nifty!

1. Create a new empty Software Instrument and with **Open Library** checked, and go to **Synthesizers | Classics | Dream Dancer**.

2. This loads a patch in Logic Pro X's most sophisticated synthesizer, the ES2, with some plugins, and it sounds really good.

3. On its channel strip fader in the Inspector, you will find MIDI FX. Hold the mouse down and go to **Logic | Arpeggiator**, and it opens:

Figure 5.8 – The Arpeggiator

Play single notes or chords, and listen to the default preset in **Live mode**.

While playing, drag the knob left to **Slow** or right to **Fast** and listen to how it changes the rate. You can also hold the mouse down on the rate filed to change it.

To the right of the **Rate** knob are a series of buttons.

The functions of the buttons are described in the manual, which can be accessed in the **Help** menu:

- **Up**: Plays from the lowest to the highest note in consecutive order and restarts when all the keys are played.

- **Down**: Plays from the highest to the lowest note in consecutive order and restarts when all the keys are played.

- **Up and down**: Plays from the lowest to the highest note in consecutive order, then plays from the highest to the lowest note, and restarts when all the keys are played.

- **Outside**: Plays the highest note, then the lowest note, then plays the second-highest, and then the second-lowest note, and so on. The arpeggio restarts when all the keys are played.

- **Random**: The played note order is randomly generated and can include duplicate notes.

- **As Played**: Plays all notes in the order they were played, then restarts.

Notice that each one has 4 variations and that it can play a range of 1–4 octaves.

With the **Latch** button disengaged, you hear the arpeggiator as long as you are holding down the keys. With **Latch** engaged, it keeps playing until you strike other keys.

In the **Pattern** tab, if you scroll down to **Grid**, or in the preset menu at the top of the plugin, you will see tons of patterns. You can also draw in your own steps in **Grid**.

One of my favorite features in **Live mode** only becomes visible if you click the disclosure triangle at the bottom, and that is **Silent Capture**. Check it and play some chords, and you have quickly created your own pattern.

The **Options** tab gives you additional controls that are really useful, especially for note length, for me.

The **Keyboard** tab allows you to choose to snap to keys and scales, while the keyboard split allows you to set ranges of your keyboard controller that generate arpeggiation and those that do not.

The **Controller** tab allows you to map MIDI CCs for your performance.

In my view, **Arpeggiator** is just great, giving you all kinds of creative options. If you compose techno or EDM, I suggest you spend a lot of time with it.

CREATING PATCHES

You can easily create very interesting sounds with Software Instruments and even save them in the Library. **Summing Stacks** is the key.

CREATING A LAYERED PATCH WITH SUMMING STACKS

Summing Stacks give us the power to create complex patches with multiple Software Instruments and save them in the Library to be used with any project.

I want to create a classic grand piano with a **Rhodes Electric Piano** patch. It's easier than you might think:

1. Create two empty Software Instrument tracks with **Open Library** checked.
2. In the first one, load a piano of your choice.
3. In the second one, load an electric piano of your choice.
4. Arm the two and play and listen to the sound. Cool, I know that sound!
5. **Shift**-select the two Track Headers.
6. Under the **Track** menu, go to **Create Track Stack**, or press **Shift + Command + D**.

It will ask you whether you want to create a Folder Stack or Summing Stack. If you click the **Details** disclosure triangle, you will see descriptions of each. Clearly, we want the Summing Stack.

You now have a Summing Stack for a playable layered instrument that you can save in the Library, but before you do, you might want to consider some more adjustments:

1. Adjust the relative volumes with the volume sliders on the individual instruments.
2. Adjust the panning of the two instruments, one panned a bit to the left, the other a bit to the right, to make the sound wider.
3. Next, **Ctrl** + click the icon to give it a more suitable icon.

In the Library window, click on **Save** and name it. There will now be a `User Patches` folder in your Library, and you can load this patch into any Software Instrument track in any project.

CREATING A SPLIT LAYERED PATCH WITH SUMMING STACKS

This is a variation that can be a lot of fun. Let's say that I want to be able to play a vibraphone with my right hand and an upright bass at the same time. No problem, the steps are the same as what we just did:

1. In the first channel strip in my Summing Stack, I chose **Mallet | Vibraphone**.

2. In the second channel strip in my Summing Stack, I chose **Bass | Upright Studio Bass**.

Now, when I play the Summing Stack, I hear both throughout the range, which is not what I want.

In the Inspector, the second section is the Track inspector. Changes here affect the entire track, not just a region.

In here, I can adjust the key range that this instrument plays.

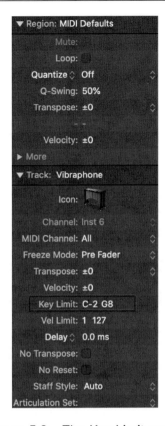

Figure 5.9 – The Key Limit range

I want this vibraphone to play from C3 to G8, so I double-click on the field and, making sure that I am only selecting **C-2**, I type in C3.

Moving to the upright bass, I do just the opposite, naming the top note in the key range B2, and the note just below C3.

Now, when I play my Summing Stack, I have it split just where I want it, and can save it in the Library.

Very cool!

Stevie Wonder said "*just because a record has a groove don't make it in the groove*," and he was right. Groove Tracks will help you make your parts feel great together.

GROOVE TRACKS

Groove Tracks is a way of making your regions groove together that works with either audio or MIDI regions. I am going to demonstrate it to you with MIDI because that is where I personally find it most useful.

I have played in a fretless bass part that has some **Quantize** settings that are pretty specific, and it feels great. Then I played a kick drum part and it is close in feel to the bass, but not quite. This is where **Groove Tracks** really shines.

If you **Ctrl** + click on **Track Header Components**, you can scroll down to add **Groove Track** to the Track Header:

Figure 5.10 – Adding Groove Track to the Track Header

Since the bass is to be the guide, in the bass' Track Header, I will move the mouse to the left and see that there is a yellow star that I can check.

After I do that, a blank checkbox appears on all other tracks. In this example, I only have the drum kit. When I check that checkbox, I am telling the drums to follow the feel of the bass, which is what I want. Works like a charm!

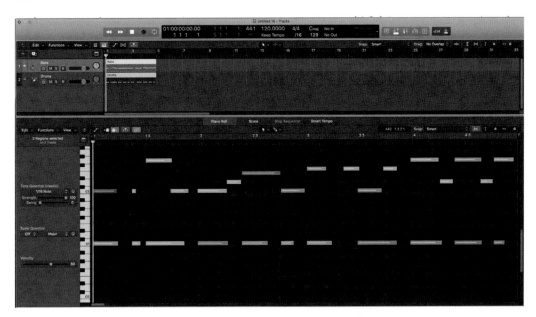

Figure 5.11 – Groove Tracks applied

SUMMARY

You have now been introduced to Logic Pro X's array of Software Instruments and have seen the various MIDI editors.

The importance of MIDI **Recording Preferences** and how they behave with non-Cycle and Cycle recording has been explained. You now can record MIDI in a number of different ways and correct its timing by quantizing. As you have learned, MIDI is not just notes but CCs as well, which you will want to record frequently.

The **Arpeggiator** adds that classic synthesizer touch, while you can individualize your sound by created layered and split patches in the Library with Summing Stacks.

Groove Tracks gives your music a tight feel that you will love.

In the next chapter, we will become familiar with step entering in the **Piano Roll** editor when you don't want to play live. This includes how to change notes pitch, length, velocity, scale, and quantization in the **Piano Roll** editor. We'll add MIDI CCs in the **Piano Roll** editor and take a brief look at the Step Editor.

6 STEP ENTERING AND EDITING MIDI

Obviously, not everybody is a good keyboard player. Even if you are, there may be musical parts you want to create that would be better served being programmed rather than played in. This process is called **step entering** and you can do it in a number of ways and then edit it to your heart's content. While you can step enter in any MIDI editor, the **Piano Roll** editor is the most user friendly and popular choice.

Specifically, this chapter covers the following topics:

- Step entering in the **Piano Roll** editor
- Using the **Step Input Keyboard**
- Entering MIDI controller steps in the **Piano Roll** editor
- A brief look at the Step Editor

STEP ENTERING IN THE PIANO ROLL EDITOR

Logic comes with a dazzling array of software instruments. Yes, there are lots of great third-party software instruments as well, but I suggest you become conversant with the Logic content before you reach for your wallet.

I will use a **Harp** for this task:

1. Open a new project with an empty Software Instrument with **Open Library** checked, and then go to **Orchestral | Harp** and click on it to load it.

2. Press **P** to open the **Piano Roll** editor and, not surprisingly, it's blank because there is no MIDI region with content yet.

3. If you drag the mouse over the keyboard you see on the side, you will hear the notes.

Let's begin with a simple arpeggiated phrase. Notice that the **Command Tool** defaults to the **Pencil Tool**, which is what we want.

With the **Command** key held down, click on the grid to the right of **C2**, and a note is created. If you hold the mouse down on it, the help tag tells you that it is **0 0 1 0**, a sixteenth note. But for this exercise, let's change it to an eighth note:

1. Position the **Pointer Tool** at the end of the note and it changes to the **Resize Tool**.

2. Drag it to the right until the **Help** tag shows **0 0 2 0**, an eighth note. The **Pencil Tool** will now default to creating eighth notes.

3. Now create three more, **E2**, **G2**, and **C3**. Now we want to create two quarter notes, **G2**, and **E2**.

4. Pencil in another **G2** and again, drag it to the right, this time until the **Help** tag shows **0 1 0 0**, a quarter note. The **Pencil Tool** will now default to creating quarter notes.

5. Pencil in another **E2**.

6. Play and listen. Very nice:

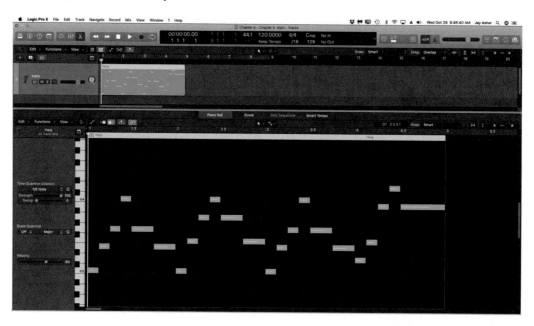

Figure 6.1 – Step entered notes in the Piano Roll

We can continue entering notes this way, but there is a shortcut:

1. Select all the notes in the **Piano Roll** by pressing **Command** + **A** or rubber-banding (dragging the mouse) over them.

2. In the local **Edit** menu, scroll to **Repeat | Once**, or press the **Command** key.

3. We may want to change the E2s to F2s and the G2s to A2s on the repeat. Select the E2s in bar 2 and hold the **Option** key and press the up arrow on your computer keyboard, and they transpose up a half-step.

4. Select the G2s in bar 2, hold the **Option** key, and press the up arrow on your computer keyboard twice, and they transpose up a whole step.

5. Select all the notes in the **Piano Roll** by pressing **Command** + **A** or rubber-banding over them.

6. In the local **Edit** menu, scroll to **Repeat | Once**, or press the **Command** key.

7. Bar 3 is just like bar 1, and that's fine, but let's change bar to **D2 G2 B2 D3 B2** and make the **G2** a half note.

8. Select the first note in bar 4 and, using the **Command** key, make it a **D2**.

9. Press the right arrow to advance to the next note and change it to an **G2**, then the next note to a **B2**, followed by a **D3**, and another **B2**.

10. Select the last note and delete it.

11. Select what is now the last note, position the **Pointer Tool** at the end of the note, and drag it to the right, this time until the **Help** tag shows **0 2 0**, a half note.

    Pretty good, but maybe the entire part should be an octave higher?

12. With all the notes selected, press both the **Option** and the **Shift** key with the up arrow and they transpose the entire part up an octave.

That sounds better, but pretty mechanical. Let's fix that. Press **D** on your computer keyboard to open the **List Editors** area, choose the **Event List**, and the problems are clearly visible:

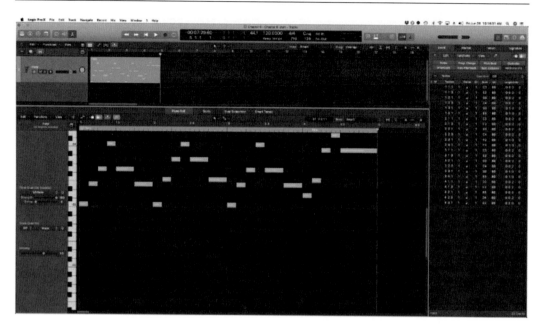

Figure 6.2 – Mechanical sounding step entered notes in the Piano Roll and Event List

For starters, they are all the same velocity. I want the first note in each bar to be a little louder. I can **Shift**-select the **C3** and **D3** on the **Piano Roll** keyboard for this purpose.

Because this is Logic Pro, there are a few ways to adjust this.

THE VELOCITY SLIDER

If you don't see the **Velocity** slider and the other items in the local Inspector, go to the local **View** menu and **Show Local Inspector**. You should see this:

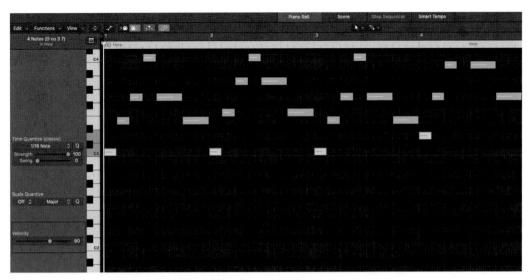

Figure 6.3: The Velocity slider in the local Inspector

If you drag it to the right, we will see the velocity increase and the color change to become more red.

THE VELOCITY TOOL

Let's change the **Command Tool** to the **Velocity Tool** by clicking on the **Pencil Tool** and pressing **V** or scrolling down to the **Velocity Tool**. Now let's make the last two notes of each bar a bit louder with the **Velocity Tool**:

1. **Shift** + select the last two quarter notes in bar 1.
2. In the local **Edit** menu, go to **Select | Same Subposition** or press **Shift + P**, and now the last two notes in every bar are selected.
3. Hold the **Command** key and drag upward on any of the notes, and they all increase their velocity and change color. Dragging down makes them softer.

Continuing in this fashion, you can make them more human-sounding, as you can see here:

Figure 6.4 – Adjusted velocities

SCALE QUANTIZE

This does just what you think it does. I will quantize the pitches of selected notes to conform to scales and modes:

Figure 6.5 – Scale and mode choices for Scale Quantize

I rarely use it, but you should experiment with it, as you may love using it:

1. Choose a scale.
2. Select the notes you wish to **Scale Quantize**.
3. Press the **Q** button and the notes conform to the selected scale or mode.

TIME QUANTIZE

You can also quantize the time on any notes you select in the Piano Roll's local Inspector by making your duration choice, adjusting the **Strength** and **Swing** if you so desire, and pressing **Q**. Notice that it says **(classic)**:

Figure 6.6 – Time Quantize in the Piano Roll

Something I did not yet show you with **Quantize** in the Region Inspector parameters is named **Smart Quantize**:

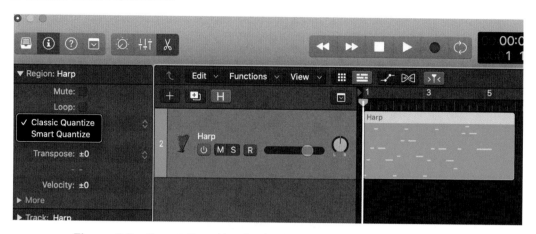

Figure 6.7 – Smart Quantize in the Region Inspector parameters

You may find that you don't need to bother with the **Advanced Quantize settings**, that just switching from **Classic** to **Smart** makes it human enough. If you change it in the Region parameters, it also changes in the Piano Roll local Inspector, which gives you the option of performing it on chosen notes rather than the whole region.

I have a talented friend who never quantizes at the region level, only in the **Piano Roll**, while I usually do. Horses for courses, as they say.

In this example, however, no quantization is necessary because it was step entered, not played. In fact, if anything, I want this to be more human.

USING THE STEP INPUT KEYBOARD

The **Step Input Keyboard** is often overlooked, but it is a gem. If you go to the **Window** menu and scroll down, you will see that you can open it:

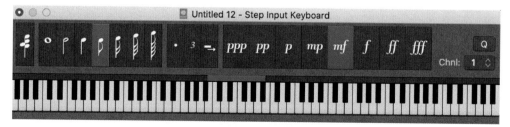

Figure 6.8 – The Step Input Keyboard

Notice that you can choose the note duration you wish to enter on the fly, including dotted notes and triplets, chords, and you can choose the dynamics as well. This is perfect for our next task, which is to create a glissando at **5 3 1 1**, culminating in a whole note chord:

1. Use the **Go To Position** command key, which is the forward slash next to the right **Shift** key, and type in **5**, then press the spacebar, then **3**, and press **Enter** or **return** to move the Playhead to **5311** (The **Go To Position** key command is my favorite.).

2. Select the 64th note at mezzo piano (mp).

3. Starting with **C4**, play a chromatic scale up to **B4**.

4. Select the **Chord** and **Whole Note** buttons, and **forte (f)**.

5. Play **C5**, then **E5**, then **G5**, then **B5**, to create a major 7th chord that lasts four beats.

6. **Shift** + select the notes in the chord and press the button that has both a rest and a right arrow, and the chord now is a two-bar chord. (If no notes are selected, it advances the Playhead to create a rest for the last duration you entered.)

Here is another nice feature. If you double-click on the MIDI in button, next to the green MIDI out button, you can now change a note pitch from your MIDI controller, and if it is velocity sensitive, it will also change the velocity:

Figure 6.9 – MIDI in/out buttons in the Piano Roll

We have come a long way, but a look at either the **Piano Roll** editor or the **Event List** reveals that the timing is still robotic.

Logic Pro has a set of presets in the MIDI Transformer that can help, which we will now examine.

MIDI TRANSFORM

In the **Functions** menu in any of the MIDI editors, you will find **MIDI Transform**. We will begin with the one named **Humanize**:

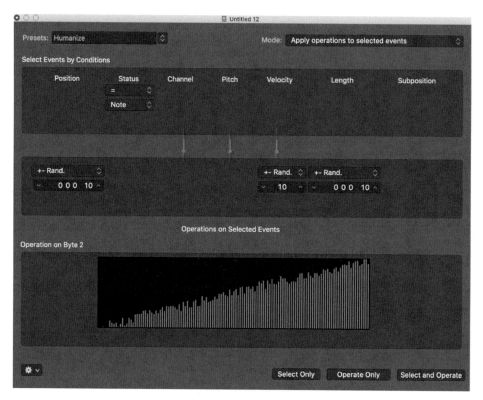

Figure 6.10 – MIDI Transform's Humanize preset

OK, that looks a little scary!

Let's figure it out. **Select Events by Conditions** is where we tell it which kind of MIDI events we want and if we want ones that are equal to it. Clearly, this preset is already designed for MIDI notes. For the **Position**, we can affect it in a number of ways that you will see in the pulldown menu, but + or- Randomization is indeed what we want. It defaults to 10 ticks either way, which is not a lot, since you hopefully remember that are 240 ticks for each sixteenth note. If you want fewer or more, you can pull down on the **10** and adjust it or double-click, but make sure you only have the **10** selected, not all the numbers in the field.

Notice you can also randomize the velocity, but I already adjusted velocities in the **Piano Roll** and think unintended musical consequences can happen with that, so I hold down the mouse on that field and go up to select **Thru** and it disappears, like magic:

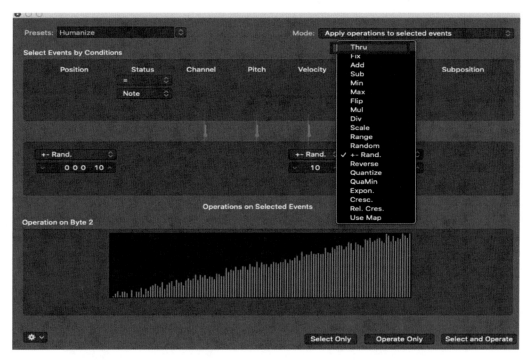

Figure 6.11 – MIDI Transform's Humanize with Length set to Thru

I feel the same way about the note length, although I doubt you would hear a ten-tick adjustment, so I do it with that field as well.

Now we need to choose from the options to **Select Only**, **Operate Only**, and **Select and Operate**. If the region is not at **1 1 1 1**, **Select and Operate** is fine, but if it is, you have to be careful not to select the first note or it could be moved to before the beginning of the project and you won't hear it. **Select Only** could be fine, but in this instance, I don't want to mess with the glissando, which contains very short notes. So, in the **Piano Roll**, I select all the notes I want to affect and press **Operate Only** and voila, it has indeed made it more human sounding by randomizing the positions a little. I can even press **Operate Only** a second time and it does it more.

Let's solve another problem with a different feature. The glissando is 64th notes, but I think they and the chord should have been twice as fast.

TIME HANDLES

In the **Functions** menu, select **Time Handles**. Nothing appears to happen until you drag over some notes, but once you do, you see them appear, all in blue:

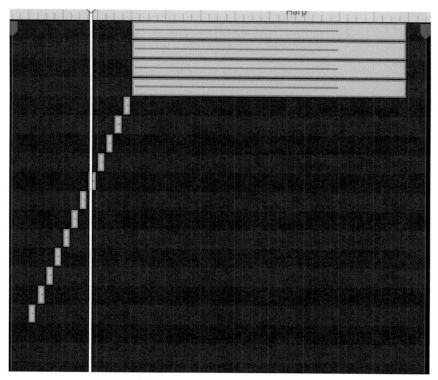

Figure 6.12 – Time Handles

Grab the right Time Handle and drag it significantly to the left, and now the notes play a lot faster! Press **Command + T** to toggle the Time Handles off, and it does not undo what you did with them.

This sounds pretty good, and I don't think you would know that it was step entered and not played live.

ENTERING MIDI CONTROLLER STEPS IN THE PIANO ROLL EDITOR

I think it would be cool for the glissando to crescendo. We can do this in the **Piano Roll** editor with velocities.

CREATING A CRESCENDO BY MIDI VELOCITY

Press the **Automation** button to the left of the MIDI in button or press **A**. By default, unless you have been editing another MIDI **Continuous Controller (CC)**, it will show the velocities of the notes.

If you hold the mouse down in the bottom of the editor just before the first note in the glissando and drag up diagonally to the velocity of the chord, you will create a crescendo:

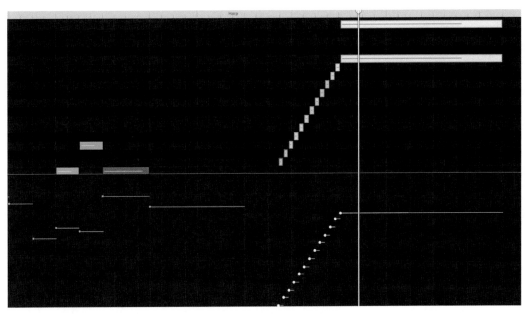

Figure 6.13 – Note velocities

To raise or lower them after the fact, select the notes in the **Piano Roll**, and use the **Velocity** slider.

CREATING VIBRATO WITH MODULATION

The harp sound is not going to be affected much by vibrato, so let's use the Library to change it to a sound that will be. Open the Library by pressing **Y**, and navigate to **Synthesizers | Classics | 80's Wave Synth**.

In the **Automation/MIDI** field, change from **Note Velocity** to **Modulation**, which is MIDI CC:

1. Drag the mouse down to the bottom of the window, right at the beginning of the region so that it says **0**.

2. Just before the first quarter note at beat 3, click the line to create a control point.

3. Right next to it, click again to create another control point.

4. Drag the second control point up to **110**. Play and listen to the effect the modulation has on the sound.

5. Just before bar 2, add two more control points close together and drag the second one back to **0**.

We have now created the following MIDI Region modulation automation by adding control points:

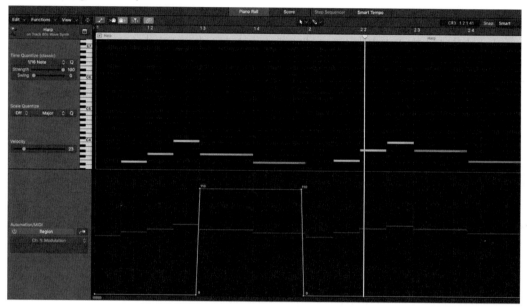

Figure 6.14 – Modulation control points

Great! You want to do the same thing at bar **2 3 1 1**, but do you have to go through all that again? No, you do not.

6. **Shift** + select the four control points.

7. Hold the mouse down on the first control point.

8. Hold the **Option** key and drag it to the desired position to copy it. Remember to release the mouse before you release the **Option** key.

That's all there is to it. You can proceed in this fashion for pitch bend or any MIDI CC you wish to automate.

A BRIEF LOOK AT THE STEP EDITOR

One of the most common complaints I hear from Logic users is that we cannot see multiple automation lanes in the **Piano Roll** editor. **Logic Pro X** has another editor that does allow it, but for reasons I cannot understand, people have not taken to it.

In earlier versions, before 10.5., you would have seen it where you now see the **Step Sequencer** tab, but it has been devalued and now you must find it by going to the **Window** menu:

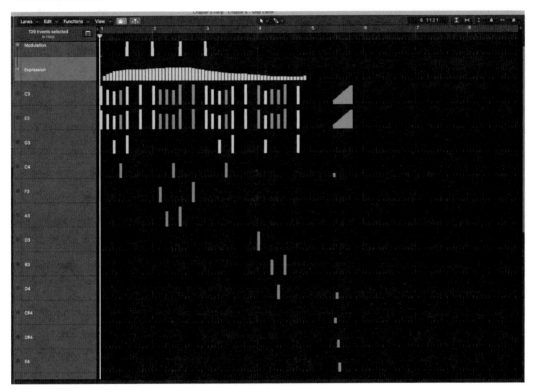

Figure 6.15 – The Step Editor

If it intrigues you, then it is well explained in the manual.

SUMMARY

You have now been introduced to **step entering** in the **Piano Roll** editor and editing you can do in the Piano Roll's local Inspector. You now are familiar with just how valuable the **Step Input Keyboard** is for these tasks, either alone or in conjunction with your MIDI keyboard. You can enter MIDI Continuous Controllers in the **Piano Roll** editor, and you know how they affect the sound. While it is not widely used or appreciated, you now know about the **Step Editor** and why you may want to consider using it.

In the next chapter, we will become familiar with Logic Pro X's Drummer, its newly revamped Drum Machine Designer, Percussionist, as well as the new Drum Synth and Drummer loops, all designed to get you the realistic drums or drum machine style arrangements you want for your project.

7
LOGIC PRO X'S DRUMMER

I am not prone to hyperbole, nor am I a fan of marketing hype, but I truly believe that Drummer was and continues to be a game-changer for beginners.

Do you know what a real drummer actually plays? I did early on, because my dad was a drummer and my first gigs were with him, but if you don't: your Drummer has arrived!

Specifically, this chapter covers the following topics:

- Drummer and the Library
- The arrangement global track
- Customizing a Drum Kit Designer drum kit
- Drum Machine Designer
- Drum synth
- Drummer loops

GETTING FAMILIAR WITH DRUMMER AND THE LIBRARY

Open a new project and select **Drummer** from the **New Tracks Dialog** window to create a Drummer instrument. While it defaults to the **Rock** genre, if you hold the mouse down on that field, you will see that there are other choices. For now, let's go with **Rock** with **Open Library** checked.

What you now have is a **Drummer** region, with the **Drummer editor** open, and in the **Library**, you will see the genre choices and multiple drummers within each genre with descriptions of the drummers, and in the **Sounds** section, a bunch of different drum kits:

Figure 7.1: A new project with a Drummer created

> **NOTE**
> The "hipper than thou" crowd made merciless fun of the
> descriptions when Drummer first appeared, but they are accurate
> and helpful.

The default **Rock** drummer is **Kyle**, and he plays a kit called **SoCal** and a preset called **Half-pipe**. Notice that with this choice, **Drummer** changes the project tempo from **120 bpm** to **110 bpm**, a tempo Logic deems appropriate for the genre. If you have, however, already employed a MIDI region in the project before opening a **Drummer** instance, it won't.

In the top left of the **Drummer editor**, you can see an arrow that if you click on, cycles the **Drummer** region:

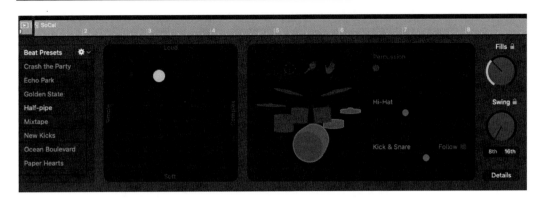

Figure 7.2: Drummer editor cycle arrow

In doing so, and while it is playing, you can change the presets, hear the difference, and check out the XY pad and drum kit area to the right and see how it changes the display. Personally, I am digging **Ocean Boulevard**, so let's go with that:

1. Zoom in on the **Drummer** region and as it is playing, what you see is that it is playing a kick drum, snare drum, and hi-hats, and that is also what you see in the drum kit in the lower-right part of the editor.

2. In the XY pad, drag the puck around from **Loud** to **Soft** and from **Simple** to **Complex**, and listen to how what the drummer is playing changes and how it updates the display in the **Drummer** region.

3. There are eight *increments* that change the pattern of **Kick & Snare**, so listen to those. Then do the same for **Hi-Hats**.

4. Click on either the cymbals or the toms and the hi-hat grays out; you only hear the selected kit pieces, and not the grayed out ones.

Why? Because **Drummer** is imitating a real drummer, and unless your drummer magically grew more hands, they can't play them all at the same time!

This is why I say that not only is **Drummer** a great way to produce realistic drum parts but it will also educate you about what a real drummer actually plays.

In the **Library**, while still in the **Rock** genre, choose another drummer and a warning appears:

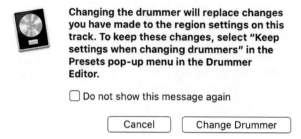

Figure 7.3: Drummer settings warning message

Eventually, you will want to check **Do not show this message again**, but you might want to wait a while before you do that, until you are more experienced with **Drummer**. For now, we don't care, so you can just change the drummer. When you do, you will see that it also changes the drum kit. I suggest you spend some time changing throughout the drummers in the **Rock**, **Alternative**, and **Songwriter** genres.

Notice that it also changes the tempo, dramatically in some cases, such as the **Punk Rock** drummer **Max**.

What if you don't love **Max** for the song you are working on, but love the sound of the **East Bay** drum kit he is playing?

If you hold down your mouse on the arrow next to the gear in **Beat Presets**, you can check **Keep drum kit when changing drummers**, and that is precisely what will happen:

Figure 7.4: Keeping the drum kit when changing drummers option

Let's agree for now that we dig **Gavin** (his description is funny) playing the **East Bay** kit. We can now press **Y** to close the **Library**:

1. Choose the preset named **The Factory**.

2. Turn the **Fills** button all the way to the left and **Gavin** no longer plays any fills. Turn it to the right and it increases the number of fills he plays.

3. By turning up the **Swing** button, you can either swing 8ths or 16ths.

4. Click on one of the three **Percussion** symbols to add them (I know, a real drummer can't do that, but consistency is overrated).

5. Click the **Details** button and three more choices appear.

Let's talk about **Feel**. If you come from the east coast of the United States, even if you keep excellent time, you probably play a little on top of the beat, aggressively. If you come from Los Angeles on the west coast, you probably lay behind the beat a bit (think E Street Band versus The Eagles). If you turn on the metronome while Drummer is playing and drag around that dial, you will immediately hear what I am talking about.

Ghost notes are small syncopations with the kick and snare that real drummers play, but unless the pattern is complex, you probably won't hear them, although with the dial is set to less or more, you can minimize or maximize the number of them.

The **Hi-Hat** dial can be set to open and close automatically, simulating the behavior of how hard a real drummer presses down on a hi-hat pedal. You can also, though, set it to your preference. Once you set these to your liking, you can click the **Details** button again to return to the main display.

I will now assume that you have the drummer you like playing the kit you like and have made this first **Drummer** region the way you like it.

Time to create a second **Drummer** region:

1. Hold the mouse down immediately to the right of the **Drummer** region and you will see a **+** sign.

2. Click it and a second identical region is created.

3. You can then proceed to alter it in the **Drummer editor** to your heart's content.

Well, that's all fine and dandy, but I want to create an entire song. Don't worry, you can, and we will explore some ways next, beginning with a global track.

ARRANGEMENT GLOBAL TRACK

If you go under the **Track** menu to **Global Tracks**, or press **G**, you can toggle **Global Tracks** on/off. If you press **option + G**, you can configure them, and the only one we need for these tasks is **Arrangement Global Track**. Dragging the bottom line of the track allows you to enlarge the field, making it easier to see.

Now, we are ready to use **Arrangement Global Track** to create **Drummer** regions. Delete the two drummer regions so that we can create regions from scratch:

1. Click the **+** sign in **Arrangement Global Track**, and by default, it creates an 8-bar-long intro Arrangement marker.

2. Repeat that process and now it creates an 8-bar verse. I decide that I only want a 4-bar intro, so I grab the lower right-hand corner and resize it to 4 bars, and now the **Verse Arrangement** marker goes to bar 5.

3. Repeat this process 8 more times, and you will probably have **Intro**, **Verse**, **Chorus**, **Bridge**, **Outro**, **Outro**, **Outro**, **Outro**, **Outro**, and **Outro**, which is not at all what you want, I'm sure.

4. Hold the mouse down on the word **Bridge** and change it to **Verse**.

5. Hold it down again, go to **Rename**, and make it **2nd Verse**.

6. Change **Outro** to **Chorus**.

7. Change the next **Outro** tag to **Bridge** and resize it to 16 bars, to incorporate a solo.

8. Change the next two **Outro** tags to **Chorus** and leave the outro as **Outro**. Resize it if you want it longer.

You now have something like this:

Figure 7.5: Arrangement markers created in Arrangement Global Track

Are you ready for some magic? Right-click in the **Tracks area** grid next to the track at bar 1 and select **Populate with Drummer regions**, and it populates the entire Arrangement track with Drummer regions!

You then can go into each Drummer region and adjust them for how you want them to sound.

CONVERTING A DRUMMER REGION INTO A MIDI REGION

Listen to the chorus and you may hear a crash cymbal at the beginning. Want to get rid of it? You can't. Oh wait, yes, there *is* a way – convert the Drummer region into a MIDI region:

1. **Ctrl** + click or right-click on the Drummer region:

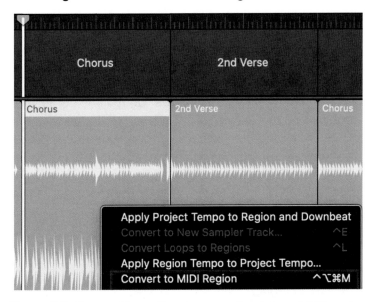

Figure 7.6: Converting a Drummer region into a MIDI region

2. The **Piano Roll** editor opens, and you see the notes and the kit piece names.

3. Click the **Collapse** button right next to **View** in **Piano Roll** and now you will see only the kit pieces that have notes played. In my case, I see two **C#2 Crash Left** notes.

4. Click on the kit piece name and it selects them. Now, hit **Delete** and they are gone.

Now, you could **Ctrl** + click and convert it back to a drummer region. I wish that I could tell you that if you do, the drummer region now reflects your edit, but it doesn't.

The other advantage of converting the drummer region into MIDI is that you can use it with any third-party drum libraries you own that do not map to general MIDI. The only thing you lose is the ghost notes.

CUSTOMIZING A DRUM KIT DESIGNER DRUM KIT

Now that you understand how Drummer works, let's explore all the ways you can change the drum kit itself.

The **East Bay** preset in the **Library** opens a drum kit with an **EQ**, compressor, and bus send to a reverb. If you press the letter **B**, the **Smart Controls** for this preset open.

Here, you will see an easy way to adjust levels within the kit, turn off kit pieces, and adjust the amount of compression or turn it off. The **Tone** knob relates to the **EQ**, and the **Room** knob affects the amount of bus send to the reverb.

I suggest you cycle a Drummer region and click on the **FX** plugins to open them, then resize them on your screen by grabbing the lower right-hand corner. Now, adjust the **Smart Control** knobs in real time, listening to the changes in the sound and observing the changes you see in the plugin windows. Fifteen minutes of doing so will teach you more than I can about processing drum kit sounds in 200 words in this book:

Figure 7.7: Smart Controls with the drum kit

Within each kit are some optional kit pieces. If you press the mouse down on the kick drum, the default choice appears, as well as two other kick drums. Each one gives you the ability to retune it, dampen it, or make it more open sounding, and increase/

decrease the gain. The same is true of the snare drum. There are no options for the toms, hi-hats, or cymbals. Hmmm!

PRODUCER KITS

As you can see, the **EQ** and compressor are applied to the kit, so their settings apply to the entire kit. That may be fine for down-and-dirty quickie demos, but it is not the kind of control you really want to have when you want to mix seriously. We will be discussing that in great detail in *Chapter 14, Mixing Your Project in Logic Pro X*.

What we really need instead of a stereo kit is a multi-output kit. In Logic Pro, this is called a **Producer Kit**. It contains the **Drum Kit Designer** software instrument with **aux channels**. Aux, short for auxiliary, channels are destination points for bus sends and multi-output software instruments (essentially, this is a **Summing Stack**, which we discussed in *Chapter 5, Recording MIDI*):

1. Press **Y** to open the **Library**.

2. Scroll down to **Producer Kits** and click the disclosure triangle to reveal them. You will see that they all have **+** next to them, which means they will use the **Drum Kit Designer** with kit pieces already assigned to come up on its separate aux channels, to give you control over their level and add plugins to the individual kit pieces, as well as control how much of the room sound you hear, leak from microphones, and overhead mics.

3. Select **East Bay +**, close the **Library**, and press **X** to open the mixer.

4. Click the **East Bay +** disclosure triangle and now you will see the entire **Producer Kit**:

Figure 7.8: The East Bay+ Producer Kit in the Mixer

But wait, there's more! Back in the **Drum Kit Designer** interface, click on the kick drum and notice how now there are many, many more kick drum choices for this kit. Ditto for the snare. And also, now we have additional choices for the toms, hi hats and cymbals – all with the options to tweak them.

Once you have made your choices, you can save the drum kit in the **Library** with another name and you now have it for every Logic project.

Even the best drummer only has two hands and two feet, so adding a percussionist brings a lot to the table. Let's see and hear how.

ADDING A PERCUSSIONIST

Let's add a percussionist, because there is nowhere that says you can only use one Drummer instrument:

1. Click the **+** at the top of the track list and choose **Drummer | Percussion**.
2. It defaults to **Isabella**, who plays **Latin Percussion**, and because we have created the arrangement markers, it populates the whole song.
3. There are three **Percussion** sets to choose from, but if you scroll down to **Producer kits**, you will see more.

4. There are also **Performance** patches that change what you hear without actually changing anything in the **Drummer editor**.

Amazing, but what if I want to add to what Drummer creates by playing in my own tom fills, for instance, turning off the fills in the Drummer regions?

You will not see a record button on a **Drummer channel strip**. They are not playable instruments. But we know that they use **Drum Kit Designer**:

1. Click the **+** at the top of the track list and choose **Software Instrument | Drum Kit Designer** with **Open Library** checked.

2. Load the **East Bay** kit (stereo should be fine for this).

Now you can play in your own tom fills or whatever else you like. Best of both worlds, if you ask me.

Drum Machines were very popular in the '80s, with models such as the Roland CR-78, 707, 8080, 909, and those from Yamaha. The LinnDrum had a different approach, trying to sound more like real drums. Roger Linn, its creator, then partnered to create the Akai MPC 60, which took drum machines to a new level.

Eventually, though, after a while, their popularity diminished until Hip Hop pioneers, looking for a cheap or even free rhythm source, discovered them at pawn shops and in trash cans, made some hits with them, and then the drum machine was back with a vengeance!

DRUM MACHINE DESIGNER

Logic Pro long ago added their software instrument emulation of a classic drum machine called **Ultrabeat**. Ultrabeat in turn became the engine of **Drum Machine Designer**. **Drum Machine Designer** has received a significant upgrade in 10.5, with a lot more kits, some of which even include guitar, piano, and bass sounds, and now it uses Logic Pro X 10.5's Quick Sampler as its basis rather than Ultrabeat, which is a significant improvement in capability, so you are getting on board at the right time:

1. Press **Shift** + **Command** + **N** to open a new project, and again create a Drummer channel strip, this time with **Hip Hop** as the genre.

2. Everything you learned with **Drum Kit Designer** in terms of the **Library**, **Drummer region**, and **Smart Controls** applies with DMD as well.

3. Let's go with **Anton** and change **Electronic Drum Kit** to **Hybrid Knock**.

4. Press **Y** to close the **Library** and **X** to open the mixer.

5. In the Mixer, under the **View** menu, uncheck **Follow Track Stacks**. This allows you to see all the **aux channel strips** in the Mixer by pressing the disclosure triangle while leaving the **Track Stack** closed in the track list.

Here, you can see DMD in all its glory:

Figure 7.9: Drum Machine Designer hybrid knock

Notice that in the upper right-hand corner of the Mixer, I have clicked the tab for **Wide Channel Strips** to see the names better.

Like the **Producer Kits** with **Drum Kit Designer**, this is a **Summing Stack**, but instead of auxes, it has instances of the new Quick Sampler, which I will go into more in *Chapter 9, Working with Sampler, Quick Sampler, and Auto Sampler*. Click on each one in the Mixer and you will see that they each have a loaded sample.

Drum Machine Designer has its **Smart Controls** built right into the interface that affects the whole kit:

1. Cycle the region and tweak them; listen to how the sound changes.

2. Click on a kit piece, however, and you will see that you have options. It defaults to the **Q-Sampler Main** tab. For now, just toggle between **Classic** and **One Shot**. **Classic** plays the sample only for as long as you hold down the key. **One Shot** plays the entire sample, regardless of how long you hold down the key.

3. Switch to the **Q-Sampler Details** tab and here you will see the sampler

controls that allow you to tailor the sound. If you have some experience with the pre-10.5 version, I think you will find that this is indeed an upgrade.

4. Switch to the **Pad Control** tab and now you will see some **Smart Controls** that only pertain to that kit piece.

5. Play a kit piece and open the **Library** and wow, you have a ton of choices for a snare sound.

DRUM MACHINE DESIGNER EDITOR

Anton changed the **Logic Pro X** project tempo to 85, but I want it a bit brighter, so I'll double-click on the tempo in the LCD and change it; but when I play it against the click, that sure doesn't sound like 100 bpm to me, it sounds like half of that.

The answer to this and some other things lies in the **Details** button of the DMD editor:

1. Open the DMD editor, by either double-clicking on the region, pressing **E** to open the editor, or pressing the editor button in the control bar and it looks pretty much like the DKD editor, with some different icons to reflect that they are electronic sounds, rather than realistic drum sounds.

2. Click on the **Details** button and this, however, looks quite different from DKD. Notice that **Auto half-time** is checked. Uncheck it, and now you will hear the region playing at 110.

The reasoning is that **Hip Hop** is almost always fairly slow, but if you want somewhere in between, unchecking this and adjusting the tempo will get you where you want to go. I settled for 90 bpm.

You will see a bunch of **Complexity Range** sliders here as well. They allow you to adjust how complex each individual kit piece's part is, despite where the puck is in the XY pad.

The original drum machines were very mechanical, locked strictly to the grid. Later ones had the ability to make it less hard quantized and to vary a bit each time it played through the pattern. DMD's **Humanize** and **Phase Variation** knobs emulate that behavior.

Let's switch genres to **Electronic**:

1. Drag the **Track Header** to the left and it goes poof! It also asks you to create a new track.

2. Choose **Drummer** with the **Electronic** genre and with **Open Library** checked.

3. It defaults to **Magnus** playing the **Big Room** electronic set.

4. It also changes the tempo to **145** because EDM, Techno, Trance, and so on all tend to be at fast tempos.

Everything you learned about DMD with **Hip Hop** applies here as well.

DRUM SYNTH

Then there is **Drum Synth**, another playable software instrument:

1. Click the **+** at the top of the track list and choose **Software Instrument | Drum Synth** with **Open Library** checked.

2. Here, you will see your choices for playable electronic drum sounds.

Combining drummers and playable software drum sounds gives you an incredible ability to quickly create fantastic drum and percussion sounds for almost any genre once you are proficient with the workflow.

DRUMMER LOOPS

Finally, we have **Drummer Loops** in the **Loop Browser**. If you open the **Loop Browser**, you have the ability to filter in/out the type of loops you see listed. Here, I have unchecked all but **Drummer Loops**:

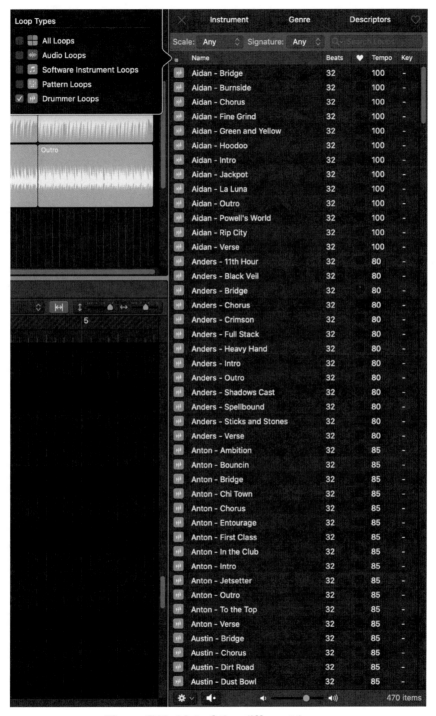

Figure 7.10: List of the different loops

As always in the **Loop Browser**, you can winnow it down even more by choosing a genre and a descriptor.

With **Drummer Loops** (and other drum loops), you can create an entire song's drums and percussion quickly and easily by dragging them into the Tracks area as well.

So much power, so much flexibility, so easy to use. Ladies and gentlemen, Logic Pro X 10.5!

SUMMARY

In this chapter, you were introduced to Logic Pro X's amazing Drummer and the drummers and drum kits in the **Library**.

You have learned how to customize the drum kit and now know why I recommend you use the **Producer Kits**. Yes, you have percussionists to play with your drummer. When you want to add **Hip Hop** and **EDM** drum machine sounds, **Machine Drum Designer** is just the ticket, while the playable **Drum Synth** option allows you to play in your own parts. Also, as you learned, in the **Loop Browser**, there are **drummer loops** for drag-and-drop drum part creation.

In the next chapter, we will become familiar with 10.5's brand-new Step Sequencer and how to creatively use it. Also, you will learn how to integrate it with **Drum Machine Designer**. **Pattern Browser** gives you a place to alter existing patterns, or create your own, and save them. The latest additions to the Apple Loop Browser are **Pattern Loops**, which, like all Apple Loops, you can drag and drop from the Browser for part creation.

8 LOGIC PRO X'S STEP SEQUENCER

Programmable step sequencers have been around for a very long time, in analog synths and drum machines. If you have ever played a kick or snare part into a drum machine, for instance, you have programmed a step sequencer. (For that matter, if you have ever created steps in Ultrabeat, you have done so as well.)

Until 10.5, though, Logic Pro did not have a proper one, but they do now!

Specifically, this chapter covers the following:

- The Step Sequencer
- The Pattern Browser
- Pattern Loops

GETTING FAMILIAR WITH THE STEP SEQUENCER

Open Logic Pro and choose **New** from **Template** and you will see that with 10.5, in **Project Chooser**, we have a new category called **Tutorials** and that there is a tutorial for the Step Sequencer. Let's begin by employing this project:

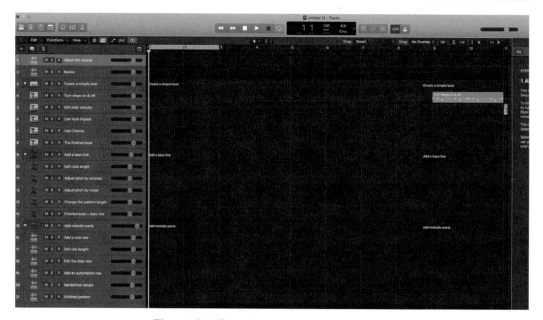

Figure 8.1: The Step Sequencer tutorial

As you can see, there are 21 tracks. Each has notes in the Note Pad. In the upper right-hand corner of the Note Pad, there is an arrow you can click on to move to the next entry.

I suggest that you spend some time with this project over a period of time as you work with the Step Sequencer to gain a deeper understanding if you find this feature attractive for what you want to accomplish musically.

But you don't need me for that, so let's open a new project with an empty software instrument channel strip, with **Open Library** checked. Navigate to **Electronic Drum Kit** and select **Brooklyn Feels**.

Click on **DMD** in the channel strip in the inspector to open the interface, and either play up chromatically from your keyboard starting at **C1** up to **D#2**, or click on the kit piece icons in the interface and listen to the very cool sounds.

We have worked with MIDI regions with software instruments, including Drum Machine Designer, and Drummer regions with Drummer, but we have a new kind of region called a Pattern Region for use with the Step Sequencer.

PATTERN REGIONS

Create a four-bar Pattern Region either by selecting it in the local **Functions** window or by **Ctrl** + clicking or right-clicking in the Workspace at bar 1 and selecting **Create Pattern Region**. Immediately, the Step Sequencer editor opens, with **16 Steps**:

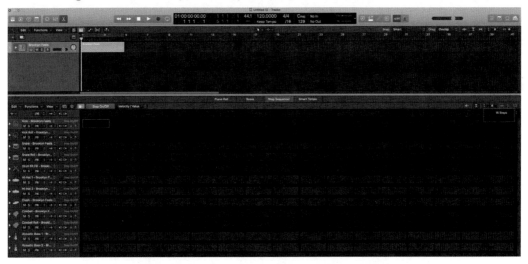

Figure 8.2: The Step Sequencer editor

Here you see rows, each with **16 Steps**. Because we chose a DMD kit, the rows are named by the kit pieces rather than the MIDI notes.

Alternatively, you can create a pattern region by pressing **E** to open the MIDI editors, choose the **Step Sequencer** tab, and then click on any step in any row and it creates a four-bar Pattern Region.

Let's explore:

1. In the upper right-hand corner, change to **64** steps. Depending on how big your screen is, you will see more or fewer of the steps.

2. Directly above it are two icons that adjust the width of the steps. Click on the larger icon and now you see four *pages* with **16** steps each that you can scroll through.

3. For now, let's return to **16** steps.

   The default for the **Pattern Region** is 16th note steps, but as you can see, you can change the Step Rate:

Figure 8.3: Step rate selection

4. You can also assign different step rates for individual Rows:

Figure 8.4: Individual row step rate selection

5. If you hold down on the **Velocity/Value** field in the header of the **Step Sequencer**, you will see there are lots of controls for the Rows. Back in the Row headers, clicking on the disclosure triangle to the left of the kit piece icon gives you something similar to **Global Tracks**, where you can choose to view these Subrows by clicking the **+** or **X**:

Figure 8.5: Subrows

CREATING STEPS IN THE PATTERN REGION

Like all MIDI regions, a Pattern Region follows the Logic project tempo:

1. Set the tempo to whatever tempo you like and click in some steps. Play and listen as it plays through one time.

2. Grab the **Pattern Region** by the lower right-hand corner, and with **Resize** tool, drag it to 8 bars; now, just like a Drummer region would, it copies those notes in the **Pattern Region** and we hear it repeat for that duration.

3. Adjust the velocities of the steps either by clicking **Velocity/Value** and dragging down/up in the step or by opening the disclosure triangle on the Row and dragging up/down on the **Velocity** Subrow.

Adjust the **Gate** time of some of the notes in the same manner.

You can now move, copy, and shorten any **Pattern Region** you create in the Tracks area. One issue you need to be aware of, though: if, in the Step Sequencer, you shorten the number of steps, those steps go away. Changing it back to more steps does not restore those steps.

> NOTE
> This is a bug to be fixed in a later update.

You can pick the direction the pattern plays back, but even better, you can pick the way each individual Row plays back and move them by increments of one step to the left and one to the right. Your choices are as follows:

- **Forward**: Steps play from left to right.
- **Backward**: Steps play from right to left.
- **Ping-Pong**: Playback alternates between left to right and right to left.
- **Random**: Steps play in an undetermined order:

Figure 8.6: Row playback and rotate row steps selectors

EDITING ROWS AND SOUNDS

If you want to re-order the Rows in the Step Sequencer, it works exactly as it does in the Track List. Hold the mouse down in the middle of the **Track Header** and just drag it up or down to your desired location.

If you want to copy, duplicate, clear, or delete a Row, right-click or **Ctrl** + click or use the key commands:

Figure 8.7: Editing Rows

THE STEP SEQUENCER LOCAL INSPECTOR

Directly above the **Step Rate** value for the Pattern Region, you will see the familiar circled letter "I" that turns on the local inspector. It has three tabs for three hierarchies: **Pattern**, **Row**, and **Step**. Like most of Logic's local inspectors, this is a very handy area to make changes in.

To the left of it is the **Pattern Browser** icon. The **Pattern Browser** is an area where you can choose and save patterns and templates.

THE PATTERN BROWSER

Let's explore using patterns from the browser with different kinds of sounds and with different kinds of Rows:

1. Create a new empty software instrument with **Open Library** checked and load any **Synthesizer Bass** sound you like.

2. Press **E** to open the MIDI editors, and if it does not default to the Step Sequencer, select it. Notice that instead of showing us kit pieces, it's showing us MIDI notes.

This is a Notes-type Row. But it is an octave higher than I want for a bass. No problem: under the **Functions** menu, you will see your transpose options and the related key commands. I could, of course, start programming in steps, as I did with the DMD track, but the **Pattern Browser** has some goodies for you.

Open the **Pattern Browser** by clicking on its icon and you should see three folders: **User**, **Patterns**, and **Templates**.

Patterns has three categories, **Bass**, **Drums**, and **Melodic**. We want **Bass**:

1. Select the top selection, **Ancient Acid**.

2. Set a four-bar cycle and while it is playing, keep pressing the down arrow each pass-through to go to the next one and audition it. There are some awesome ones.

3. All the Rows and all the Steps are green. As in other areas in Logic, pressing **Option + C** opens the color palette, and you can color each row. Under the **View** menu, you can then have it color the steps by Row colors.

4. Have fun adding and deleting steps and rows, with all the techniques you learned working with the DMD pattern.

Once you come up with something you really like, you can save the pattern in the Pattern Browser **Action** menu, or even as a template, and it will be in the **User** folder:

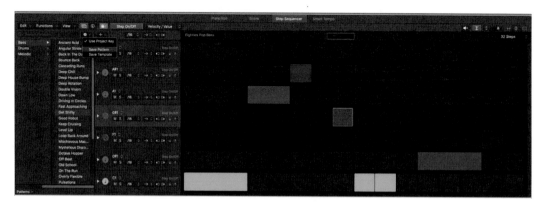

Figure 8.8: Saving in the Pattern Browser

A **Melodic**-type Row is similar to the Note type, just geared more to the kind of sounds you heard with classic step sequencers in analog synthesizers. Again, create an empty software channel strip with **Open Library** checked, load a synth patch, and in the Pattern Browser, go to **Melodic** and choose a preset. All that you learned in the two previous patterns applies here as well.

Automation Rows can be created to automate any settings in the plug-ins.

Click **+**, scroll to **Automation**, and choose a setting to automate, as I have done here:

Figure 8.9: Creating an Automation Row for automating a setting

Now I have an **Automation** Row for the **FilterBlend** of the **ES2**:

1. Under the **View** menu, I recommend you select **Zoom Focused** to see the Row better, and with **Velocity/Value** selected, just click in values in each step.

2. Play and listen and you hear it jump from value to value, but you would probably like the steps to be smoother.

3. Open the local inspector and select **Row**.

4. In **Automation** mode, it defaults to **Latch**, but if you hold the mouse down, you can change it to **Slide**, which *slides* from value to value. **Latch** just jumps to each value.

(This use of the word *Latch* did confuse me, frankly, because it isn't like Latch in Track and MIDI region automation, which you use in real time with the project playing.)

PATTERN LOOPS

Finally, there are also **Pattern Loops** in the Loop Browser, as you can see in the filtering options:

Figure 8.10: Pattern Loops in the Loop Browser

As with any Apple Loop, you can simply drag it into the Workspace below the other tracks to create a region. Now you can open the Step Sequencer and edit away to make it your own.

This thing is deep! Now that you have a basic understanding, you may well want to return to the included Logic Pro X Tutorial project to further explore the new Step Sequencer.

SUMMARY

You have now been introduced to what the Step Sequencer is and how its Pattern Regions, Rows, and Steps work together. Like all the MIDI editors' local inspectors, the Step Sequencer local inspector is very helpful. You learned how to alter existing patterns or create your own and save them so that they are available to you in any project with the **Pattern Browser**.

There are three different Row types: **Notes**, **Melodic**, and **Automation**. **Pattern Loops** are the latest entry into the Loop Browser choices, for drag and drop part creation.

In the next chapter, we will become familiar with Logic Pro's Sampler, formerly the EXS24, Quick Sample, and Auto Sampler.

9 WORKING WITH SAMPLER, QUICK SAMPLER, AND AUTO SAMPLER

Logic Pro was the first digital audio workstation to include its very own software-based sampler, the **EXS24**, at a time when GigaSampler was really the only other choice. Many of its competitors still don't include a free one; you have to buy theirs.

If you used Logic before the 10.5. update, you'll recognize this:

Figure 9.1 – EXS24

Many users felt that it had gotten a bit long in the tooth, and begged for a more modern and powerful sampler, and in 10.5, they have one.

It's simply called **Sampler**, and as the French say, *vive la difference*:

Figure 9.2 – Sampler

If you used Logic before 10.5 and are used to loading patches in the EXS24 and are familiar with its architecture, comprising sampler instruments in one folder with the samples in another, you needn't worry that anything has changed that will not allow you to use your Sampler Instruments. It will all work as expected.

If, however, you are brand new to Logic Pro, let's begin by learning how to load instruments into **Sampler**. Logic Pro X has a trio of new samplers.

We will specifically be discussing the following in this chapter:

- Loading instruments into Sampler
- Working with the Quick Sampler
- Getting familiar with Auto Sampler

LOADING INSTRUMENTS INTO SAMPLER

You can load patches that work with Sampler from the Library, just as we did in *Chapter 5, Recording MIDI*.

Because the **Library** is contextual, if you have a Sampler already instantiated, you will see patches that work with **Sampler**. As you know, it will load however not only the sampler instrument but also some FX plugins, which you may or may not want.

If you prefer, hold the mouse down where you see **Factory Default** on the **Sampler** interface and scroll down to see **Factory instruments**, **GarageBand instruments**, and any third-party libraries you have purchased or instruments you created.

Scroll down to **Factory instruments** and load any instrument that interests you.

Since this a beginner's book, I am not going to go deep into all the controls that you can use to edit this sound, but notice that we see five panes:

- The **Synth** pane contains options for **global pitch**, **panning**, **volume**, and **filters** for the sound, as you will find in any of the Logic synths.
- The **Mod Matrix** pane has modulation routings to affect the sounds.
- The **Modulations** pane is where you will find the **LFO** and envelope modulators for controlling pitch, amplitude, and filters that you can route in the **Mod Matrix** pane.
- The **Mapping** and **Zone** panes are for creating and editing your own sampler instruments.

These are well covered in the Logic Pro 10.5 instruments guide that is found in the help menu. For now, you can spend some time in each and tweak and hear how it changes the sound.

Clicking on the right arrow loads the next instrument in the list, while the left arrow loads the previous instrument in the list.

The updated sampler is very nice, which is all well and good, but the thing that has me excited is its companion, **Quick Sampler**. Let's see why!

WORKING WITH QUICK SAMPLER

If you again open **Logic Pro** and choose **New** from **Template**, you will see that with 10.5, in **Project Chooser/Tutorials** is an option for for the **Quick Sampler** that you may want to spend some time with.

For now, open a new empty project and in the **Software Instrument** field, choose **Quick Sampler**. It looks like this:

Figure 9.3 – Quick Sampler

There are lots of ways to bring a sample into the **Quick Sampler** and work with it. Let's explore some of the ways.

LOADING APPLE LOOPS TO QUICK SAMPLER

The following steps will show us how to load Apple Loops to Quick Sampler:

1. Press **O** to open the **Loop Browser**.

2. Choose the loop pack called **Disco Funk**.

3. From the **Instrument** tab, select **All Drums**. I like one called **Glitter Nights Beat**. It's **16** beats long with 4 bars:

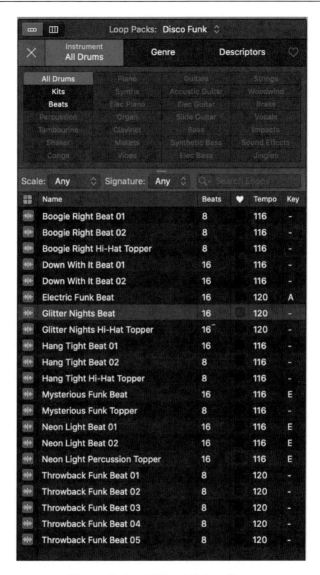

Figure 9.4 – Glitter Nights Beat

In **Quick Sampler**, we have four choices for behavior in the interface: **Classic**, **One Shot**, **Slice**, and **Recorder**. We will begin with **Classic**.

4. Drag the loop into the center of the interface and you have two choices: **Original** and **Optimized**. Since this is an Apple Loop, it will already have no blank audio at the beginning and end of it, nor will it need crossfades, so either will work. I recommend getting in the habit of using **Optimized** (if you drag it to the **Track Header**, it opens in **Slice** mode).

5. Play a note on your keyboard and it will play for as long as you continue to hold down the key, regardless of how far it has progressed in playing back the loop

6. Play different notes on your keyboard, starting with notes below middle C and then moving up past middle C. You will hear that the higher the note, the faster it plays. That is probably rarely what you want.

7. Under **Pitch**, you will see that **Key Tracking** is on. Turn it to off, and now, as the notes you play change, the tempo playback and pitch remain constant. However, if I change the project tempo in the LCD, it isn't adjusting, and we want it to.

8. Right above the **Amp** section, you will see a flex icon. Click it and **Follow Tempo** is now on and it follows the project tempo. Next to that is a speed menu, where you have a range of choices to play the loop back at multiples of the project tempo:

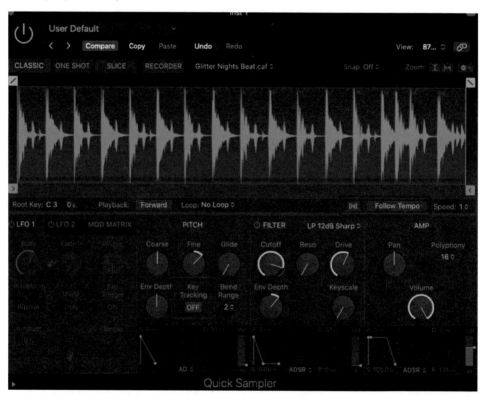

Figure 9.5 – Key Tracking off with Follow Tempo on

9. Switch the tab from **Classic** to **One Shot**. Play a note on your keyboard and it plays the entire loop all the way through, even if you don't hold down the note.

At the bottom left and right of the waveform, you will see handles that if you drag left and right allow you to resize the loop, and under the **Gear** menu, crop the sample if you wish. At the top left and right of the waveform, you will see handles, which if you drag left and right create fade-ins and fade outs. You can even change **Playback** from **Forward** to **Reverse**.

10. Switch to **Slice** mode and now you have a way to play each section of the loop with the slices mapped chromatically.

11. If you turn on **Play To End** and hit a key, it starts to play. But if you play other notes within the instrument's range, it triggers them and then resumes.

Fantastic! Return to **One Shot** for now.

In the bottom section, much like **Sampler**, you can tweak LFOs, **Mod Matrix**, **Pitch**, and **Filter**, and the **Amp** section as well. Spend some time playing around with these and you will find that it is so powerful and yet so simple. I adjusted **Fine Pitch** a bit higher, chose the **LP 12dB Sharp Filter** preset, adjusted **Cutoff** and **Drive**, and it sounds really different:

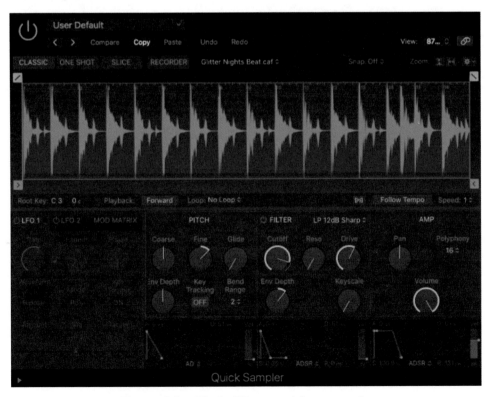

Figure 9.6 – Pitch, Filter, and Amp tweaks

Go into recording mode with **Quantize** set to **1/1** in the Inspector's **Region Parameter** box and play it 4 times by playing the trigger note once every 4 bars, for a total of 16 bars.

With it selected, press **U** to create a cycle. Now, let's add a bass!

1. Create another **Quick Sampler** instrument.

2. In the **Loop Browser**, clear the instrument selection and select **Bass**, still in the **Disco Funk Loop** pack.

3. With Logic cycling, find a bass loop that works for you. Let's choose **In The Pocket Bass**, but instead of dragging it into the workspace, drag into **Quick Sampler One Shot | Optimized**.

4. When I play it, I think it sounds great, but I only want part of the loop, so I adjust the left and right to begin at **4 3 1** and end at **11 1 1**. If dragging it doesn't get it perfectly in place, type in those numbers. Don't worry: you can double-click on each field and type in the numbers:

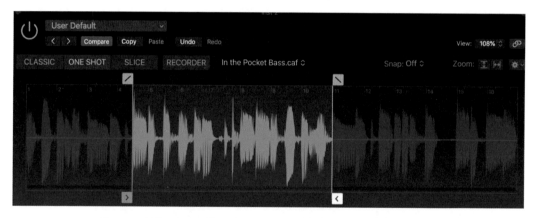

Figure 9.7 – Selecting a part of the sample for cropping

5. Under the **Action** menu, the gear symbol, crop the sample.

    Because this is a melodic instrument, I want it to have **Key Tracking** on. But doesn't that mean it will get faster if I play a higher starting note? Not to worry, as long as **Flex-Follow Tempo** is on.

6. Play in a simple part by playing a note every two bars. I played **C3** twice, **Eb3** twice, **F3** once, **G3** once, and back to **C3** twice.

IMPORTING EXISTING AUDIO FILES INTO QUICK SAMPLER

Importing existing audio files into **Quick Sampler** is really easy. To begin with, do the following:

1. Create another **Quick Sampler** track.

2. Where you see the **No audio** file loaded, choose **Load Audio File**, which opens a file selector so that you can navigate to the audio file you want.

3. It gives you the choice of **Original** or **Optimized**. Unless you know that there is no blank audio at the beginning and/or end of the audio file, I recommend choosing **Optimized**.

4. Alternatively, you can drag and drop it from the **Finder** into the interface where you see **Load**, **record**, or **drag an audio file here**.

5. Alternatively, you can press **F** to open the **File Browser** and find it and drag it into the same area.

6. Once it's in the **Quick Sampler**, of course, you have all the same options you had with the other methods.

7. All of these **Quick Sampler** instruments can be saved as **Quick Sampler** instruments; they are saved with the project if, when you click **Save As**, you check **Sampler Audio Data**, and as patches in the **Library**.

Recording into **Quick Sampler** is another way to bring samples into it, which is a lot of fun.

RECORDING INTO QUICK SAMPLER

You will need a microphone for this. If you don't have one yet, most Macs have a built-in one:

1. Choose the **Recorder** pane and practice what you want to record. If your level isn't hot enough, adjust the **Threshold** slider.

2. Press the **Record** button, and because this is **Disco**, I borrowed a play from the **Sly & The Family Stone** playbook and recorded myself saying *"Hey yeah, shaka-laka-boom!"*

3. With Logic playing, I set the quantize to ¼ in the Region inspector so that I get the timing right between the two phrases.

4. I go to **Classic** and **Coarse** pitch it down a bit to give it a deeper sound. **Classic** gives me the ability to sometimes play the whole phrase and other times just the *Hey yeah* part. And yes, I want **Key Tracking** on for this.

5. Recording the part, I play the keys as I like.

6. I added some FX, such as **EQ**, **Stereo Delay**, and a **Phaser**, and now I have the following.

Silly, I know, but fun! You can download the `Chapter 9 example.mp3` available at this link. https://github.com/PacktPublishing/Jumpstart-Logic-Pro-X-10.5

EXPORTING DRUM SLICES TO CREATE A DRUM MACHINE DESIGNER TRACK

Again, this is super simple:

1. Return to the first **Quick Sampler** where we brought in the **Disco** drum loop and go to **Slice** and under the **Action** menu, then select **Create Drum Machine Designer track**.

Step 2? There is no step 2; that's all there is to it, and you can save it in the **Library**.

Quick Sampler is exactly that, a quick and easy tool for creating your own creative, playable sampler instruments, and it's my favorite new feature in 10.5.

Next up is **Auto Sampler**. **Auto Sampler** has actually been around for quite a while. It was originally created by a company called **Redmatica**, who made a number of products that worked with the EXS24, Kontakt, and other sample engines. Eventually, however, Apple bought them out and hired the lead developer, Andrea Gozzi.

Auto Sampler became a feature of MainStage, Apple's live performance app for MacOS, iOS, and iPad iOS. Now, with 10.5, we have it in Logic Pro X as well.

GETTING FAMILIAR WITH AUTO SAMPLER

Auto Sampler is a tool to convert patches in hardware keyboards and other software instruments into playable sampler instruments in Logic. Have a favorite sound in your Yamaha Motif that you would like to have? How about a sound from a Kontakt library that is resource-demanding?

Sounds great, and it is. A couple of caveats, though:

- It isn't going to always sound exactly like your hardware synthesizer. Your synthesizer has filters and FX that will not translate to the **Auto Sampler**.

- If your example Kontakt library has a bunch of different articulations or *true legato* (recorded intervals going from one note to the other), **Auto Sampler** will not capture that because Sampler does not have that capability, at least not at the time of writing this chapter.

- Depending on your choices and how large the instrument is and how fast your Mac is, it can take quite a while.

Still, it is very useful, and I have created several instruments already with it.

I am going to use an instrument from the **Kontakt Factory Library**, so as to not annoy any library developers for Kontakt who may not be thrilled by this (it is not illegal, so long as you don't try to sell your auto-sampled instruments):

1. I will load from **World | 2 Recorders | High Whistle**.

2. In an Audio FX slot, scroll to **Utility** and instantiate **Auto Sampler**.

3. If you want your own FX to be part of the auto-sampled instrument, add them to insert slots on the channel strip before the **Auto Sampler**.

It opens and you see the interface:

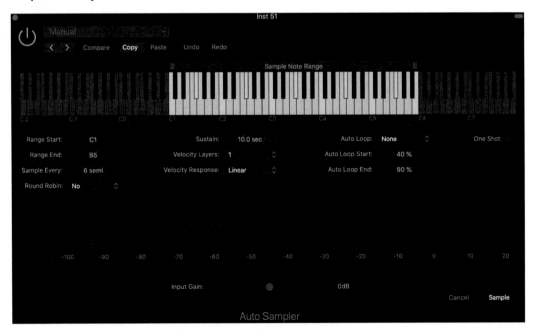

Figure 9.8 – Auto Sampler

It's pretty easy to understand. You set **Range Start** and **Range End** to the range of the instrument. In this instrument, it is **F1** to **D4**.

It helps to know something about the instrument. Most developers tell you in their literature how many round robins and velocity layers the instrument has, for instance. The lower the number of semitones, the longer it will take but the better reproduction, but not all sampled instruments themselves use a different sample for each semitone. If the developer did not actually use that many samples but looped and re-pitched some the **Auto Loops** options, this may be something you will want to explore. The sustain time for mallets or drum hits obviously does not need to be as long as a flute because the sound decays faster. So, there is a certain amount of trial and error.

Once you have made your choices, press **Sample** and it starts. You may want to turn your speakers down and go grab a snack!

When it is finished, if you open **Sampler** and scroll to the presets, you will see that you now have an **Auto Sampled** folder, where your auto-sampled instruments now reside and you can load them. Of course, you can also save them in the Library.

A really cool feature is that it also works with **Summing Stacks**, so if you want to combine two violin patches from different libraries into one playable sampler instrument, combine them in a **Summing Stack**, and load **Auto Sampler** in the Audio FX slot on the **Summing Stack**, and away you go!

There you have it, the powerful new trio of samplers in Logic Pro X 10.5.

SUMMARY

You have now been introduced to **Sampler**, which is the revamped version of Logic's **EXS24** sampler. You have learned about the power and ease of use of my favorite new feature, **Quick Sampler**. **Auto Sampler**, a feature of MainStage that allows you to convert patches from hardware keyboards or other software instruments and their libraries, is now also part of Logic Pro X.

In the next chapter, we will become familiar with working with **Live Loops** and its cells and scenes. We will also see how to play cells and scenes live, as well as record and edit cells and scenes.

10 WORKING WITH LIVE LOOPS

All of the major digital audio workstations err...*borrow* from each other. 10.5's new **Live Loops** feature clearly owes a debt to Ableton Live. **Live Loops** is a way to create music in a non-linear fashion, organizing cells in a grid. If you are familiar with Ableton Live, then you already know about the concept of composing by triggering cells and scenes.

Specifically, this chapter covers the following topics:

- Starter Grids
- Understanding Cells and Scenes
- Editing cells
- Creating scenes from cells
- Playing cells and scenes live
- Recording cells and scenes into the Tracks area
- The new Remix FX multi-effects plugin

As with the other new features, 10.5 includes a tutorial for **Live Loops** that you may well want to spend some time with. For now, though, let's begin by employing one of the many starter grids that are provided for you.

UNDERSTANDING CELLS AND SCENES WITH A STARTER GRID

Open **Logic Pro X** and choose **New** from **Template**, and you will see 17 starter grids. You can choose any one you like, but I am beginning with the starter grid named **Elevated Beats**:

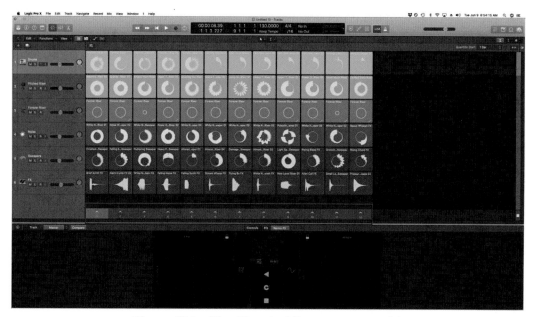

Figure 10.1 – The Elevated Beats starter grid

Well, this looks like nothing I have ever seen in previous versions of Logic, and when it was leaked on social media, I made a fool of myself by saying that I thought it was created in Photoshop!

Here, you can see six tracks in the track list. Each track has 12 colored cells that are organized into 12 scenes, which are horizontal columns of cells that can be triggered together. The numbered scene trigger buttons are at the bottom of the grid. In the preceding screenshot, below them, you can see the **Smart Controls**, with a new group of plugins named **Remix FX**.

Sometimes, the best way to learn about something is to just try it. Let's listen to some cells:

1. Mute tracks 2–6 and select a cell in track 1.

2. You will see a Play arrow appear. If you click on it, you will hear the cell. Press the spacebar to stop.

3. Listen to the different track 1 cells.

4. Unmute track 2 and now you will hear the cells in both tracks playing together.

5. Proceed in a similar fashion with the other tracks.

Now, let's trigger some scenes, which you see laid out at the bottom of the grid. Simply click on the **Scene Trigger** button on the arrow above the **Scene number**. Notice that in this starter grid, each cell and the first five scenes are 8 bars long. Scenes 6–12 take 4 bars to play all the way through.

Key commands are especially helpful with Live Loops. Let's look at some.

Press **Option + Return** and you will see that the transport begins to progress through the project, but you don't hear anything. That is because it has taken the cells out of the queue. Pressing them a second time puts them back in the queue.

With all the cells no longer queued, you can add cells to the queue by **Ctrl** + clicking them and using the shortcut menu to add them to the queue. You can also add scenes to the queue by **Ctrl** + clicking the **Scene Trigger** buttons.

Right next to the **View** menu are the **Show/Hide** buttons for the Live Loops grid and the **Tracks** view:

Figure 10.2 – Show/Hide buttons

You can switch between them or see both. The key commands are user-friendly:

- **Option + L** for **Show Live Loops Grid** only
- **Option + N** for **Show Tracks View** only (presently empty)
- **Option + B** for **Show Live Loops Grid** and **Tracks View**
- **Option + V** to toggle between **Live Loops Grid** and **Tracks View**

If you have both the **Live Loops** grid and **Tracks Area** showing, there is an adjustable **Divider column**, and at the bottom is the **Grid Stop** button:

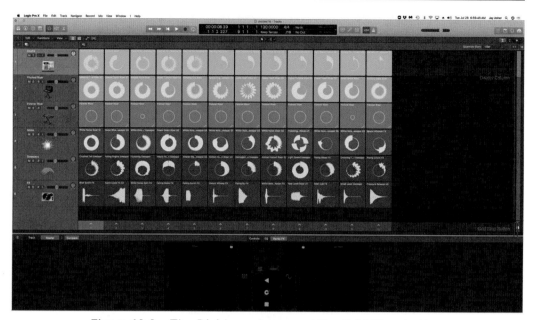

Figure 10.3 – The Divider column and the Grid Stop button

You now have a basic understanding of the relationship between cells and scenes and how they are triggered. Let's move on to editing a cell.

EDITING CELLS

Open the Inspector and select a **cell**, and now you will see the **Cell inspector**:

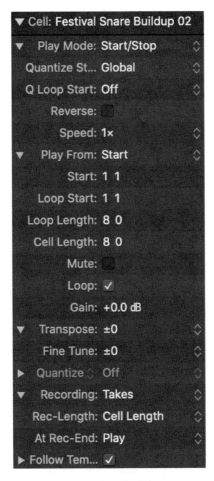

Figure 10.4 – The Cell inspector

Wow, that is a lot of control! We will cover these briefly, as you will find experimenting with them more informative than what we can cover in this book.

For **Play Mode**, you have three choices:

- **Start/Stop**: Clicking a cell starts and stops playback.
- **Momentary**: Cells play as long as you click and hold them.
- **Retrigger**: Clicking an additional time starts playback from the beginning of the cell.

Quantize Start can be set globally in the **Quantize Start** menu at the top right of the **Live Loops** grid, or for a scene by **Ctrl** + clicking the **Scene Trigger** buttons, or for individual cells. Selecting a specific **Quantize Start** value allows you to determine, if the cell is not triggered from the beginning, where it starts. **Quantize Loop Start** only matters if you have **Play Mode** set to **Start/Stop**.

Reverse, **Speed**, the **Play From** choices, and the rest are all pretty much self-explanatory, until we get to the **Recording** options, which we will explore a little later in this chapter.

There is a **Cell Editor**, but since when you select a MIDI cell you see **Piano Roll**, with an **Audio cell**, a waveform, a **Pattern cell**, the **Step Sequencer**, a **Drummer cell**, and the Drummer editor, for me, this isn't really a distinct editor; it just opens various editors with some slight differences. Since you are already now familiar with those editors, I will not go into the Cell Editor further here.

Next up, we'll learn how to create scenes from cells.

CREATING SCENES FROM CELLS

I think we will be better served by creating a new **Live Loops** project for this:

1. Go to **New** from **Template** and open a new **Live Loops** project.

2. With both the **Live Loop** grid and the **Tracks area** open, you can see that I have added a bunch of Apple Loops to the **Tracks area** that I like:

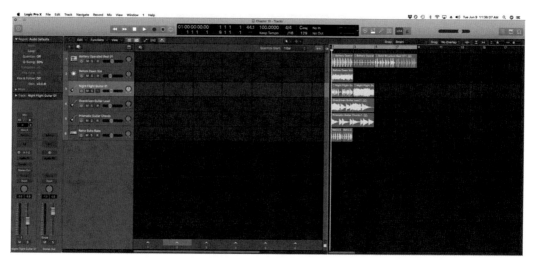

Figure 10.5 – Apple Loops added to the Tracks area

3. Add the **Apple Loops** to empty **cells** in the **Live Loops grid** by dragging and dropping them in, and try out different combinations in the queue; I arrived at the following:

Figure 10.6 – Apple Loops added to the Live Loops grid

I have four scenes ready to be triggered. I can move or copy cells from one scene to another the same way I move and copy regions in the Tracks area, either dragging them to move or **Option** + dragging them to copy. If you drag a cell on top of another, it replaces it. I can now delete the Apple Loops from the Tracks area since I no longer need them if I choose.

While I used Apple Loops for convenience, remember, you can perform the same tasks with any audio regions.

This is great so far, but wouldn't it be awesome if I could record a software instrument part in a cell, or even a vocal sound? Well, you can, and here's how.

RECORDING INTO CELLS

I decide, crazy guy that I am, that I want to record hand claps into a cell through **Amp Designer**:

1. Create an **audio track** in the **track list**.

2. At the desired location, create a cell by **Ctrl** + clicking the empty cell space.

3. Again, **Ctrl** + click the cell and choose **Record Into Cell**, then clap your hands repeatedly for as long as you like.

Yes, it is that easy. I now decide I want to add a **Vintage Electric Piano** cell. It's the same process:

1. Create a **Software Instrument** track in the **track list** with **Vintage Electric Piano**.

2. At the desired location, create a MIDI cell by **Ctrl** + clicking the empty cell space.

3. Again, **Ctrl** + click the cell and choose **Record Into Cell**, then play your electric piano part for as long as you like.

Now that I have all my cells and scenes to my satisfaction, I want to record a performance to the Tracks area. As you will see, it isn't difficult, and you can even do this by triggering cells or scenes in real time.

RECORDING A PERFORMANCE TO THE TRACKS AREA

I have **Grid Quantize Start** set in the **Quantize Start** menu to **Cell End**. Right above the first cell in the first track is the **Enable Performance Recording** button, which if you click, turns a bright red:

Figure 10.7 – The Enable Performance Recording button

Let's begin recording:

1. Press **Option + Return** so that no cells or scenes are queued.

2. You can set your **Count-In** and **Metronome** settings to whatever you prefer.

3. Press the **Record** button in the **Transport Bar** or **R** on your keyboard.

4. If while it is recording you select a cell, **Shift + select**, or rubber-band over some cells and hit the **Return** key, it will record them as regions in the **Tracks area**.

5. If while it is recording you select the **Scene Trigger** button, it will record the cells in the scene as regions in the **Tracks area**.

Once you have completed your performance recording, right at the top of the divider line is a double-arrow icon, which allows you to switch between whether the Live Loops grid will have Track Priority or the Tracks area:

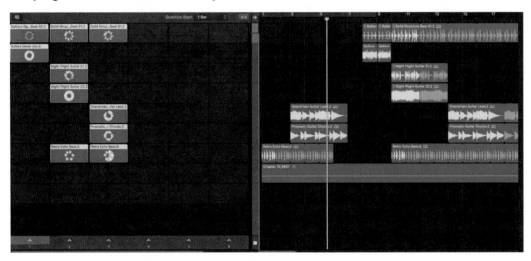

Figure 10.8 – Track Priority arrows

I am not going to lie, doing this from your computer with a mouse and keyboard does not feel as fluid as it should be. However, there are, at the time I am writing this, a couple of alternatives.

LOGIC REMOTE

There is a free companion app for the iPad and iPhone called **Logic Remote** that users have found very useful. It has been updated to incorporate all the new features and it is just great for triggering cells and scenes to record a performance in real time. If you have a reasonably robust internet connection, you are probably going to really like it.

NOVATION LAUNCHPAD AND LAUNCHKEY MIDI CONTROLLERS

For those of you who prefer the feel of hardware and have a few bucks to spare, Novation has a line of MIDI controllers in a wide price range that are great for working with Live Loops. They were originally designed to work with Ableton Live, but they now work with Logic's Live Loops as well.

With this new **Live Loops** feature, surely there are some new FX designed especially for it? You betcha. Let's take a look at **Remix FX**.

REMIX FX

In addition to its Phat and Step multi-FX, we now have Remix FX, which you will find in the **Multi Effects** folder. It is designed to be used on the stereo output, but you can use it on individual tracks or auxes as well.

Those of you who have used GarageBand for iOS will already be familiar with it. Unlike most of the Logic Pro FX plugins, these are designed to be used live, DJ style.

OVERVIEW

There are seven areas in the Remix FX plugin that you can utilize:

- **Filter**
- **Gater**
- **Reverse**
- **Stop**
- **Scratch**
- **Downsampler**
- **Repeater**

They are controlled by two XY pads, buttons, some faders, and sliders. There are dedicated **Smart Controls** mapped to it. If you open the **Smart Controls**, though, I notice that they look quite different if Remix FX is on the stereo output or on a track, but more on that in a while.

To the left side and the right side are the two XY pads, assigned to **Filter** and **Repeater**, but if you click on the words **Filter** and **Repeater**, you will see that each XY pad has a choice of six different FX that you can control from them:

Figure 10.9 – XY pad choices in the Remix FX plugin

You cannot set both XY pads to the same FX. As you choose different FX, you will see that the options of what to control with that FX update to reflect the things it was designed to do.

To the right of the left XY pad is a slider that controls **Gater**, and if you click on the icon to the right of it, you see some settings choices for a selected effect appear:

Figure 10.10 – Settings for a selected effect

If you drag the slider up and down while the project is playing, you hear the cool gating FX more or less as you drag it. Very cool.

The second slider controls **Downsampler**, either in **Classic** or **Extreme** mode.

The three buttons in between the sliders control, from top to bottom, **Reverse Timing**, **Scratching**, and **Tape Stop** to slow down all things DJs do in real time:

Figure 10.11 – Real-time DJ-style effects

There are locks to lock the pads in their current state so that you can then chose another FX to control with the XY pad. You can also unlock the locks, while reset does just that, it resets the FX.

CAPTURING REMIX FX WITH AUTOMATION

We can automate our FX for specific scenes or the entire project, either by selecting the scene to be queued in the Live Loops grid or setting a Cycle in the **Tracks** view:

1. Add the stereo output to the track list by selecting it in the **Mixer** and either assign it to an **Automation** mode or press **Shift + Command + M**. It immediately goes to the bottom of the track list and cannot be moved.

2. Assign the **Automation** mode to **Latch**. **Latch** must be used instead of **Touch** if any of the FX movements are locked, and is the best choice for this task because it doesn't snap back to the original setting when you release the mouse.

3. Put the project into play and have fun with the FX; Logic will automatically create **Automation Lanes** for every parameter you use.

4. Change the **Automation** mode to **Read**, and you are done.

The biggest disadvantage to this perhaps is that the Smart Controls that appear on Remix FX on the stereo output cannot be used for automation, so you have to do it in the plugin. But also, what if you don't want every track to have these FX, only certain ones?

The following solution kills both birds with one stone.

Select the tracks you wish to affect and change their output assignment from **Stereo Output** to an available bus by holding down the mouse on the output assignment and selecting an unused bus send. Logic creates an aux to host that bus:

1. Move the Remix plugin from the stereo output to the new aux.

2. Automate the FX to your heart's content as before in the plugin *or* from the Smart Controls.

Now, only the tracks you wish to be affected, in the parts of the song you want them to be affected, are, and you have more control by adjusting the aux.

Again, you will probably find using the Remix FX plugin more enjoyable from Logic Remote than with your computer mouse and keyboard, so check it out if you own an iPad or iPhone.

SUMMARY

You have now seen the power of the Live Loops grid as a creative tool for modern composing in styles such as EDM. By using fully editable cells, assembled into scenes, recording your own audio and software instruments cells, and dragging in existing audio or Apple Loops, you can create a unique performance, and then record it into the Tracks area. Spice it up with the new Remix FX and capture your real-time performance with them with latch automation. This may totally change the way you work.

In the next chapter, we will learn how to record without a click, yet create a tempo map, affect the timing of imported audio with relation to the project tempo, and adjust the tempo of the audio regions to match the project tempo. We will fix the timing of audio parts with **Flex Time** and the pitch with **Flex Pitch**, and use the classic technique from the tape recorder days of Varispeed to speed up or slow down a whole project.

11 WORKING WITH AUDIO FILES, TEMPO, AND PITCH

As we have already learned, changing tempo and pitch with MIDI is quite easy since MIDI is just a set of instructions. It's also, as we have learned, easy with Apple Loops since they are designed to chase tempo and keys and transpose easily.

Audio is also now similarly easy to work with, as is demonstrated by the fact that the blue Apple Loops are in fact audio loops. **Logic Pro X** gives you terrific tools for working with controlling the relationship between audio files, projects, and tempo.

Specifically, this chapter covers the following topics:

- Adjusting your project tempo to match an imported audio file
- Fixing the timing of audio parts with **Flex Time**
- Fixing note pitch with **Flex Pitch**
- Changing tempo playback with **Varispeed**

You may want to bring in existing audio files to a project and change their tempo to work with your project at the desired tempo, but there are also times when you are beginning a project when you want to start with an imported audio file from another project, and have the project tempo adjust. **Smart Tempo** makes this easy.

ADJUSTING A PROJECT'S TEMPO WITH AN IMPORTED AUDIO FILE USING SMART TEMPO

As we did with the Rubato recording, we will first start by changing the setting in the Control bar's LCD from **Keep Tempo** to **Adapt Tempo**. For this task, however, there is an additional project setting we need to attend to:

1. Go to **Project Settings | Smart Tempo**.

2. In the middle pane, change **Set imported audio files to On**. I also like to set it to **Trim start of new regions** so that the region is placed right at **1 1 1 1**:

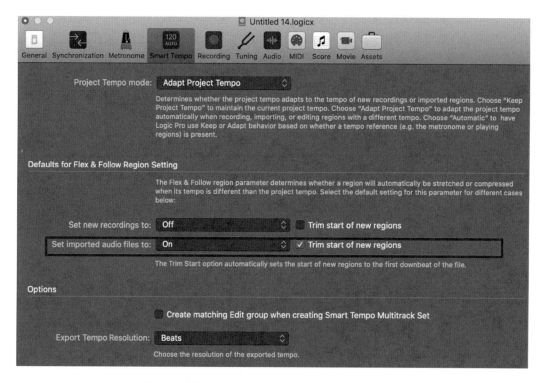

Figure 11.1 – Smart Tempo project settings

3. If I now bring in an audio file, as I am doing here with a kick drum, **Smart Tempo** analyzes the audio file's tempos and adjusts the project's tempo changes accordingly:

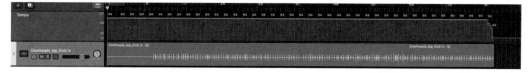

Figure 11.2 – Tempos applied to the project from an imported audio file

But what if audio files were not played that well in terms of their timing? We can fix that with **Flex Time**. Open the `Chapter 11 project`.

FIXING THE TIMING OF AUDIO FILES WITH FLEX TIME

If it's something really simple, **Flex Tool** may get the job done quickly for you. In this screenshot, if you look at the **Snare** drum, it is pretty clear that several of the snare hits are late, not hitting directly on beat 4 each time:

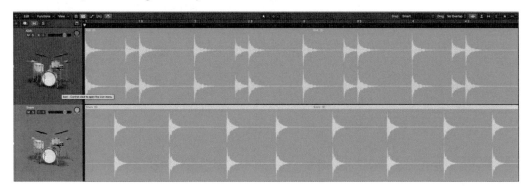

Figure 11.3 – Late snare hits

Let's fix it!

1. Press **T** and change **Left Click Tool** to **Flex Tool**.

2. Click on the region with the Flex Tool. This turns on **Flex & Follow** in the **Region** inspector.

3. Press the **Command** key, which by default switches to the **Marquee tool**.

4. Drag the **Marquee** tool over the **Snare** hit and start to move to the correct position. It changes to the **Hand** tool for that purpose.

Done – that was easy:

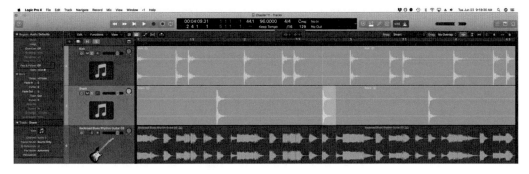

Figure 11.4 – Timing of the corrected snare hit

The kick drum is really poorly timed in multiple spots. It needs to be quantized to 8th notes, so let's use **Flex Time** in a more sophisticated way:

1. Click the **Flex** icon above the region, which enables **Flexing**, but defaults to **Monophonic**.

2. Change it to **Slicing**, because slicing works best for short notes such as drum hits:

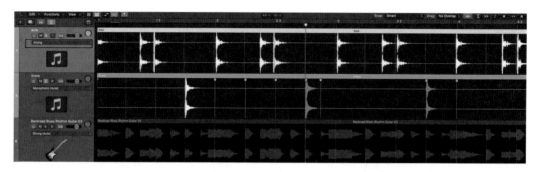

Figure 11.5 – Enabling Flex with Slicing mode

3. In the **Region** inspector, set **Quantize** to **1/8 note**.

Boom! The timing is spot on.

There are other modes in addition to **Slicing** that work similarly for other kinds of material. **Monophonic** mode is perfect for solo instruments such as a bass. **Rhythmic** can work on guitars and keyboards if the parts are simple, but for more complex parts, **Polyphonic** will probably work best. **Speed** and **Tempophone** are special effects that you probably will not use much, but feel free to try them out if you like.

FIXING THE PITCH OF A VOCAL WITH FLEX PITCH

Pitch Correction is something you may well want to do, unless you are Bruce Springsteen or Bob Dylan!

The big dogs in the pitch-correction jungle are AutoTune and Melodyne, but with **Flex Pitch**, we have a free alternative that is rather more like the Melodyne approach than the AutoTune method.

You can use **Flex Pitch** in the **Tracks** area, but I much prefer using it in the **Track Editor**, because I can have it on a second monitor; the functionality, however, is the same. I have performed a bluesy little vocal, but my pitch is a little off. I want to improve that, but not lose the bluesy nuances.

Click the **Flex** icon above the display in the **Track Editor** and change the mode to **Flex Pitch**, and you will see beams that represent each note:

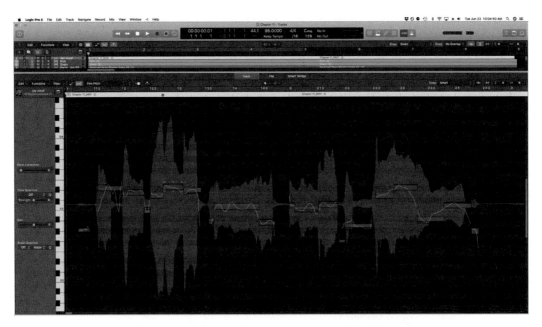

Figure 11.6 – Enabling Flex Pitch in the Track Editor

We are ready to begin:

1. Press **Command + A** to select all the beams that represent the notes.

2. Then, **Ctrl** + click on one of the notes and choose **Set to Perfect Pitch** and listen.

I am not happy with the result. Logic thinks I meant to sing some notes that are not what I was going for, plus, some of the bluesy quality is lost. Press **Command + Z** to undo it. For the notes that I do want to assign to perfect pitch, double-clicking on the note will do precisely that. But I want to take a more human approach, given the nature of the vocal. If you hold down on a note, in the middle of the beam, you will see the pitch and position. Notice that there are also three hotspots on the top and three more on the bottom.

The top three, from left to right, are for adjusting **Pitch Drift**, for leading into the note, **Fine Pitch**, for tuning, and **Pitch Drift**, for leaving the note, respectively. The bottom three, from left to right, are for adjusting the note's gain, the amount of vibrato, and the formant, respectively.

The **Formant** setting helps make the note sound more/less natural when higher or lower. Resuming my work, I decide to begin by using **Fine Pitch** to correct notes that bother me. The first note is OK, because it's bluesy, but the second note, a **D#**, sounds sharp to me, and the third note, also a **D#**, sounds flat:

1. Hold the mouse down on the mid hotspot for **Fine Pitch**; mine says **23** (cents). 100 is a semitone, so it is in fact a little sharp. I'll drag it down closer to **0** and it sounds better.

2. The third note is a D natural that is 42 cents sharp, but I was going for a **D#**. Drag the **42** up with the mouse until it is closer to a **D#** and it sounds good.

The seventh note is a C natural but it's longer and it almost sound like two pitches. For the best result, switch the **Command** + click to the **Scissors** tool and cut the beam in half, and sure enough, you will see two pitches that you can edit:

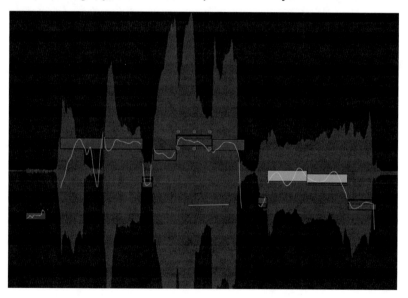

Figure 11.7 – The beam cut into two pitches

Continuing on in this manner, you can correct any pitches that bother you. You can also adjust the vibrato by dragging down on the **Vibrato** hotspot with the mouse to decrease it or drag up to add vibrato. If you have too much drifting into a note, or drifting out of a note, you can drag the hotspots to decrease the amount. You could also increase it, but I have yet to encounter a scenario where I have wanted to do this.

One thing I did on another project was to select all the beams and drag the **Formant** hotspot up a bit, which made me sound a little younger, but not unnaturally so. Very cool!

Using **Flex Pitch** takes a bit of practice, but once you are comfortable with it, you can correct a vocal very quickly. Personally, I don't like my pitch correction to be too perfect, but you may feel differently. Now we turn to **Varispeed**.

VARISPEED

Varispeed was a feature of tape recorders that is now digitally emulated in **Logic Pro X**. It was famously employed by David Seville (Ross Bagsdasarian) to create the sound of *The Chipmunks*. By singing in a lower key more slowly, adjusting the **Varispeed** made it increasingly higher and faster, giving him that signature sound.

We can use it in Logic Pro X to speed up or slow down the playback of a project without, or with, the chipmunk effect of the pitch getting higher.

I have a project loaded that I recorded at 130 beats per minute that I want to playback a little slower, or faster. Feel free to load one of your own.

First, we need to enable Varispeed. In *Chapter 2*, *Getting To Know the Logic Pro X Interface*, you learned how to customize the Control bar. Here, you can see that **Varispeed** can be added to the Control bar's **LCD** section:

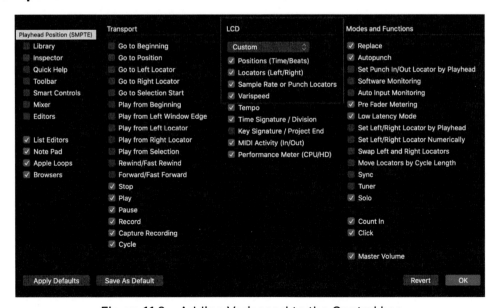

Figure 11.8 – Adding Varispeed to the Control bar

Now, on the Control bar, you will see a button with a minus and a plus sign. Clicking it turns on **Varispeed**:

Figure 11.9 – Varispeed activated

By default, it is set to **Speed Only**, no *chipmunk* effect. You can hold down on **Speed Only** and switch to **Varispeed** and **Pitch** if you want both, and even **Varispeed** and **MIDI** for when you have both audio and **MIDI** regions.

Also, by default, it shows you the percentage change when you drag up or down on that field. If you drag it down **3%**, however, you don't know what the tempo is with that percentage, unless you do the math. Holding down the mouse on the percentage field allows you to change the view to **Resulting Tempo**, which I find more useful.

3% changed my playback tempo from **130** to **126.100**. If I double-click on the tempo, I can round it off to **126**. Now, when I hit play, I hear my project playback a bit slower without the pitch changing.

Click on the **Varispeed** button to turn it off and you are back to hearing it at the original speed.

SUMMARY

We began by learning how to match a project's tempo to that of an imported audio file with **Smart Tempo**. You now know how to correct the timing of a performance with the **Flex tool** and **Flex Time**. You can tune a vocal with **Flex Pitch** and use it to alter its character by adjusting **Pitch Drift**, **Vibrato**, and **Formants**. You have read about the beginnings of **Varispeed** with tape recorders and the digital emulation of its functionality in Logic Pro X.

In the next chapter, we will explore methods for getting an arrangement ready for mixing by employing project alternatives for different versions, inserting, copying or deleting sections, and removing problematic noise so that you have cleaner audio files to mix.

12 GETTING THE ARRANGEMENT RIGHT

It is really hard for an engineer to do a great mix that has a lot of impact on the listener if the arrangement isn't right. In this chapter, we will discuss what your priorities should be and how to achieve a great arrangement.

We will discuss the following:

- What really matters in your arrangement?
- Creating a Project Alternative for different arrangements with the same project
- Adding, copying, and deleting sections with the help of locators and Skip Cycle

WHAT REALLY MATTERS IN YOUR ARRANGEMENT?

One of the most common issues I see in people's work, especially less experienced music creators, is the creation of just too many parts that they fall in love with.

I love to watch movies with commentary from the director. Sometimes they will show you a deleted scene and say that it was a great scene and that they hated to lose it, but that it hurt the flow of the movie.

The same may be true in your arrangement. You may love that brilliant synth part, but if it draws focus away from a part that matters more, or competes with it, you have to be prepared to be a little ruthless and decide that it has to go.

KNOW YOUR GENRE

If you have a song and the most important elements of it are the singer interpreting the lyrics and some lovely piano or acoustic guitar, then you will have one set of criteria. If you are doing an EDM song, your drum machine and synthesizer parts may be the things that your audience will be most interested in.

KNOW YOUR STRENGTHS AND WEAKNESSES

If your song needs a great guitar but you are not a great guitarist, you may have to either hire one or hide your guitar parts in the mix under better-played parts, even though you are the guitarist.

Again, you have to take your ego out of the decision-making process and do what is best for the song.

Let's say that you have a project you are preparing to mix, or have mixed, and you are pretty happy with it but you want to create a shorter, more succinct version. Or maybe you just want to experiment. You want to give yourself a chance to return to its present state, and pressing **Command + Z** as many times as possible may not get you there. The answer is to create a Project Alternative.

CREATING A PROJECT ALTERNATIVE

Open the `Chapter 12` project.

The process is very simple:

1. Navigate to **File** | **Project Alternatives** | **New Alternative**:

Figure 12.1: Creating a Project Alternative

2. Name the alternative.

3. Here you can see that I have created three Project Alternatives, and the third one is the active one:

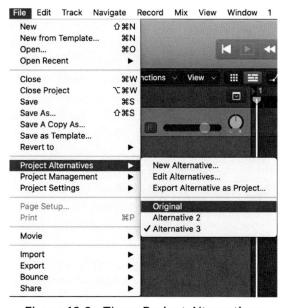

Figure 12.2: Three Project Alternatives

To return to an earlier or later version, all I have to do is select it in the **Project Alternatives** list, and it will return to the state it was in at that point. If I choose **Edit Alternatives**, I can rename or remove any I choose.

This is a great way to create different arrangements, all within the same project.

> NOTE
> Personally, I like to name my alternatives by the date and time, so when I return to an earlier or later one, I know when I last worked on it.

ADDING A SECTION TO YOUR ARRANGEMENT

Setting **Cycle locators** to define the bars that we will be working with ensures that we get the results we need for some of the tasks we will now perform.

If you decide that your arrangement needs an additional section to add to its impact, such as an a cappella intro or a guitar solo, or a drum break, it's pretty easy to create it.

INSERT SILENCE AT LOCATORS

Let's suppose that somewhere in our project we want to add a four-bar drum break using the first four bars of drums:

1. Create a Cycle for the four bars. The Cycle sets the locators.

2. Navigate to the local **Edit** menu and choose **Edit** | **Cut/Insert Time** | **Insert Silence at Locators**:

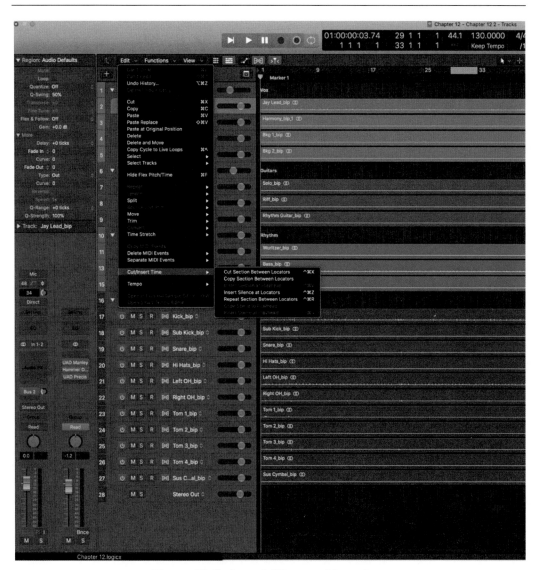

Figure 12.3: Insert Silence at Locators

3. After this is done, you will see that Logic has created four blank bars at that location:

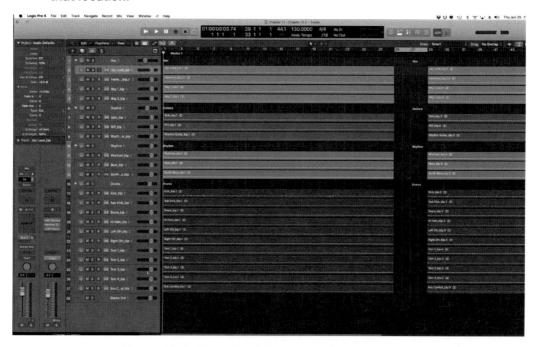

Figure 12.4: Four blank bars have been inserted

4. Holding the **Command** key to switch to the default **Marquee Tool**, swipe over the drums for the first four bars. If you press the **Play** button in **Transport** or the spacebar, you will now hear those drums:

Figure 12.5: Four-bar drums selection

5. Hold **Option** and drag them to the desired location. In this case, you may well want to set your **Snap** to **Bar-Absolute**, as was discussed in *Chapter 4, Editing Audio*:

> REMINDER
> You must release the mouse before the **Option** key, or you will move the material rather than copying it.

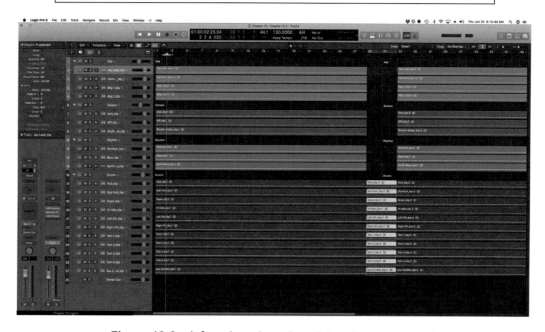

Figure 12.6: A four-bar drum break has been created

Let's explore another scenario. I want to repeat an eight-bar section of the song without vocals for a guitar solo.

REPEAT SECTION BETWEEN LOCATORS

Bars 33–41 is the material I want to have repeat for a guitar solo before bar 41 kicks in:

1. Create a Cycle for the eight bars to set the locators.

2. Navigate to the local **Edit** menu and choose **Edit | Cut/Insert Time | Repeat Section Between Locators**.

3. Turn off the Cycle by pressing **C**.

Voila, it is done:

Figure 12.7: Repeated bars have been inserted

Easy, but I do have one problem I need to fix. It repeated the section with all the regions, including the vocals, which I don't want. All I need to do is select those regions in the vocal tracks and either delete them by pressing the **Delete** key, or mute them by pressing **Ctrl + M**.

DELETING A SECTION OF YOUR ARRANGEMENT

Maybe your song is a little long for the airplay you hope to get, or a transition from one section to the next is not quite as impactful as it should be. While not all editing in the Tracks area is destructive, it helps to get an idea about what it will sound like without the deleted section.

CUT SECTION BETWEEN LOCATORS

Let's hear what your arrangement would sound like without a section. I am choosing bars 13–21:

1. Create a Cycle for the eight bars to set the locators.

2. Hold down the **Ctrl** key and the mouse on the cycled area in the Bar Ruler and choose **Swap Left and Right Locators**. This creates a Skip Cycle.

3. Press play to start playback a few bars before and note that when you reach bar 13 it immediately jumps to bar 21, skipping those eight bars:

Figure 12.8: A Skip Cycle

If you are happy with what you hear, you can proceed. You might want to create yet another Project Alternative.

4. Go to **Edit** | **Cut/Insert Time** | **Cut Section Between Locators**.

5. Turn off the Cycle by pressing **C**.

And again, it is done. Pretty easy, no? Let's do some more problem-solving.

CONSOLIDATING REGIONS AND CONVERTING MIDI TO AUDIO FILES

If you are like me, you may only record a small number of audio parts and use a lot of software instruments and plugins. Bouncing is just another term for what other applications refer to as rendering. The process creates new audio files.

Here is why you might want to consider bouncing all the parts to audio files for mixing audio files:

- You are collaborating with another musician or engineer, and they don't own all your third-party software instruments or they are working in another DAW, such as Pro Tools.

- Your computer gets bogged down with CPU demands and RAM usage.

- Many software instruments and plugins do not perform identically every time you play them back.

- When you commit a part to audio, you have fewer things to think about and can concentrate on your mixing.

- Creating a Project Alternative means you can always return to a previous version if you need to.

When time permits, this is always my preferred way to get ready for a mix. Others who do a lot of *mix-as-you-go* things may not prefer it as it limits them. (I like having limits, but I am not the workflow police.)

In the following screenshot, you see a recent song of mine with some audio and software instruments tracks:

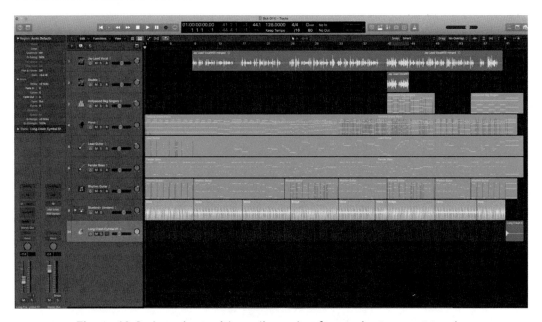

Figure 12.9: A project with audio and software instrument tracks

Logic gives you a number of options, which we will now take a look at:

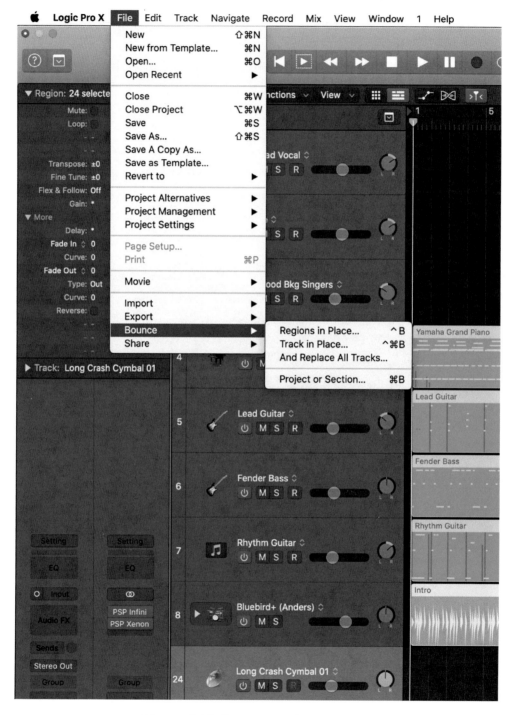

Figure 12.10: Bounce in place options

BOUNCE TRACK IN PLACE

Bounce Track In Place is great for when you want to choose which tracks you want to bounce to a new audio file while not bouncing others. It gives you a wide range of options:

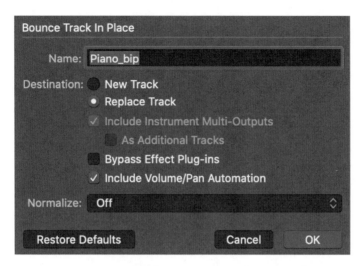

Figure 12.11: Bounce Track In Place options

As you can see, you can use the following options:

- Create a new track or replace the current track.
- **Include Instrument Multi-Outputs** as part of the audio file or **As Additional Tracks**.
- **Bypass Effect Plug-ins**.
- **Include Volume/Pan Automation**.
- **Normalize**.

There are lots of choices for you to make. I generally prefer to create a new track, bypassing the plugins, so that I can copy plugins from one to another in the Mixer by holding the **Option** key and dragging them from one channel strip or revisiting them from scratch, to another if I choose to. If you are a *mix-as-you-go* person, you may have already done some automation and panning, which we will be discussing at length in *Chapter 14, Mixing Your Project in Logic Pro X*, and *Chapter 15, Automating Your Mix*.

I *never* use **Normalize**, because when you do, you are no longer bouncing what you are hearing, which makes no sense to me.

I will generally select **Include Instrument Multi-Outputs** when using multi-output instruments, as I always do for drums, so that I have more control over the sound of each kit piece. I will choose to include them as additional tracks, so that I end up with separate audio files for each kit piece, such as kick, snare, hi-hats, and so on:

Figure 12.12: Bounce Track In Place with multi-output instruments results

In the Mixer, you see the multi-output drums, while in the Tracks area, you now see the bounced-in-place audio files for each.

If you select tracks in the track list while holding the **Shift** key, **Bounce Track In Place** becomes **Bounce Tracks In Place**, again with the same choices available.

BOUNCE REGIONS IN PLACE

This is similar to **Bounce Track In Place**, and you can use it when you want to discretely bounce only certain regions or bounce a mix of regions:

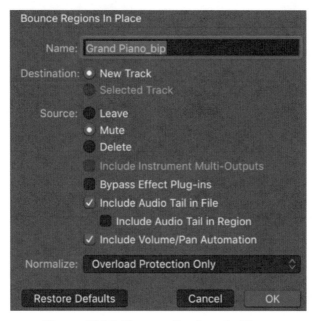

Figure 12.13: Bounce Regions In Place

This is the method I employ least often, as it just does not accomplish what I generally want to do, which is to have consolidated tracks. But, as they say on the internet, *your mileage may vary*.

BOUNCE AND REPLACE ALL TRACKS

This does exactly what it says; no selecting involved. The downside is that there are fewer options, but it does include separate multi-output instruments as discrete audio files:

Figure 12.14: Bounce And Replace All Tracks

This works well when time is a factor, but generally, my favorite is to use **Bounce Tracks In Place**, because it gives me the most control over the results.

EXPORT TRACKS AND REGIONS

Exporting instead of bouncing is an option for when you want to send audio and/or MIDI regions and tracks to another collaborator or engineer or a Final Cut Pro user, or when you want to bring them into a fresh project to work on. It's also great for archiving to guard against the day that something bad happens to your Logic project:

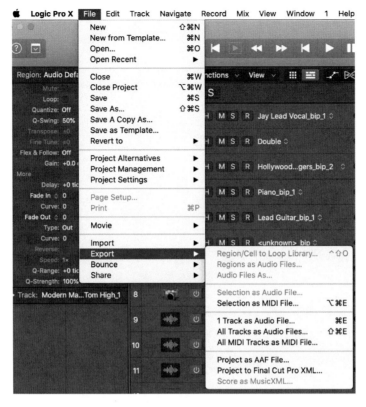

Figure 12.15: Export options

When you choose one of the options, such as **All Tracks as Audio Files**, you now see a range of choices for naming and organizing that far exceeds the bounce options:

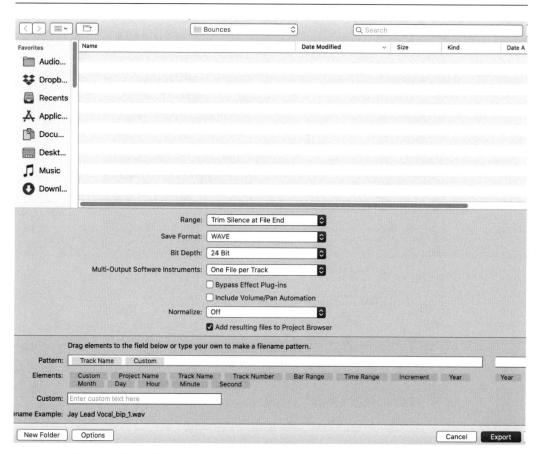

Figure 12.16: Export options with Export All Tracks as Audio Files

Wow, that is a lot of options, and many of them are fairly recent additions in Logic Pro. This is just great for ending up with audio files that are where you want them, include what you want, and are named and organized how you would like – and you can include them in your project!

This is my personal favorite, because I like control.

> NOTE
> When using summing stacks, you need to either expand them by opening them or flatten the stacks first, by pressing **Shift + Command + U.**

Rather than creating new audio files in the project, you may prefer to temporarily *freeze* tracks to free up CPU demands. In fact, some people may say, *Jay, you saved the best for last*.

FREEZE TRACKS

To use **Freeze** tracks, first we need to make the option visible. While holding the **Ctrl** key, press down your mouse in the track header and add **Freeze** to **Track Header Components**, and after you do so, you will see the little *snowflake* button:

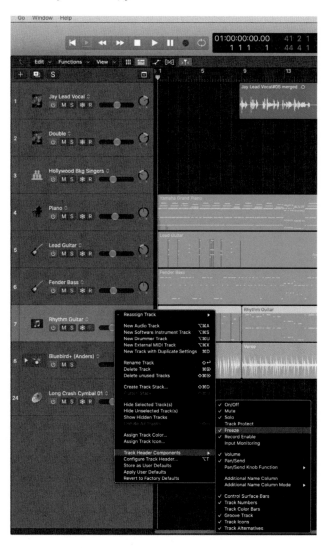

Figure 12.17: Adding the Freeze snowflake to the Track Headers

Freeze tracks, a form of offline bouncing, were first developed at a time when most Macs were considerably less robust in terms of CPU power as a way of freezing a track so that the tracks were temporarily converted to 32-bit float audio files, freeing up CPU resources.

You freeze the tracks by clicking on the snowflake buttons of the tracks you want to freeze and starting playback. While they are in a frozen state, they are not editable, but reversing the process reloads any plugins.

A lot of people still love this feature. So why don't I?

- For me, freezing and unfreezing was a momentum killer and my present computer is powerful enough that I don't need to employ it.
- It doesn't freeze multi-output instruments or summing stacks.
- The 32-bit float files it creates, oddly enough, cannot be imported into another project.

But you may well love it and choose to make it one of your Track Header component defaults.

SUMMARY

In this chapter, we learned how to get our arrangement just the way we want it by adding and deleting sections, consolidating regions and converting MIDI parts to audio files, and employing **Freeze** tracks while we do so to avoid CPU usage issues.

In the next chapter, we will learn how to organize our project to make mixing easier with folder stacks, multiple Mixer views, markers, screensets, giant displays of bars/beats, and time.

13 ORGANIZING FOR THE MIX

Organization is essential because an ounce of preparation is worth a pound of cure. Mixing is difficult, so we want to do anything we can to get our project ready to go.

We will discuss the following topics in this chapter:

- Folder Stacks in the Track List
- The Mixer's three views – **Single**, **Tracks**, and **All**
- Advantageous use of Screensets
- Creating Markers and using them for navigation
- Giant Beats and Bar display

If you like, you can either use the project from *Chapter 12, Getting the Arrangement Right*, for this or use your own.

As you can see, I have already made a good start to getting organized. There are not that many tracks and my track and region names match, and they are colored so that they are easily identifiable, as we discussed in *Chapter 4, Editing Audio*:

Figure 13.1 – A project with tracks and regions name- and color-matched

But since I am mostly now going to be working with the Mixer, maybe I don't need to see all of them all of the time. Let's see what we can do about that.

GETTING FAMILIAR WITH FOLDER STACKS

In *Chapter 5*, *Recording MIDI*, we were introduced to **Summing Stacks**, and we could well employ them here, but since all we are looking at is organization, there is another type of **Track Stack**, called a **Folder Stack**, that is well suited for this purpose.

Following my color-coding, I now want to create four Folder Stacks.

CREATING FOLDER STACKS

With all the vocal tracks selected, if I go under the **Track** menu to **Create Track Stack**, or press **Shift + Command + D**, I am given a choice between creating a **Summing Stack** and a **Folder Stack**. The description tells me that **Folder Stack** is well suited for the simple organization of tracks in the track list:

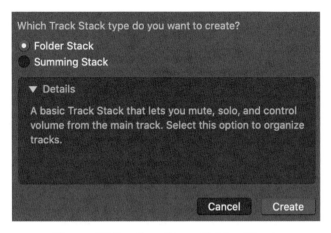

Figure 13.2 – Creating a Folder Stack

Let's begin with a **Folder Stack** for the vocals:

1. Choose **Folder Stack** and you will now have a **Folder Stack** named `Sub 1` with a waveform icon and a different color.

2. Double-click on the name in the Track Header and rename it `Vocals`.

3. **Ctrl** + click on the icon and switch to one that looks like it is for vocals.

4. Finally, open the color palette by pressing **Option** + **C** and give it the same color as the vocal tracks.

I now have a **Folder Stack** for the vocals:

Figure 13.3 – A Folder Stack

Following the same procedure, I will now create the remaining three Folder Stacks. Here is what I see with all the Folder Stacks open. You can open and close the Folder Stacks by toggling the disclosure triangle:

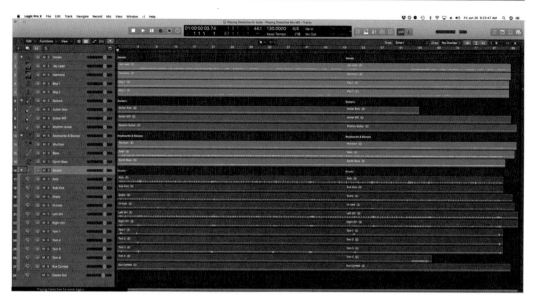

Figure 13.4 – Folder Stacks opened with the disclosure triangle

If you press **Option + K** to open your key commands and in the search file you type the word `Stack`, you will see that there are helpful key commands for toggling **Track Stacks** open and closed, two assigned, two unassigned:

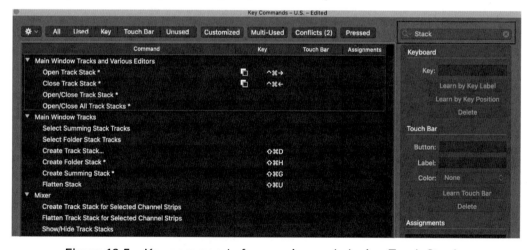

Figure 13.5 – Key commands for opening and closing Track Stacks

I actually prefer using the key commands to toggle a given **Track Stack** open/closed and all of them to toggle open/closed, so I would definitely recommend assigning a key command to those.

FOLDER STACKS AND THE MIXER

If you open the Mixer by pressing **X** on your keyboard, you will see that if the **Folder Stacks** are open in the Track List, they are open in the Mixer, and if they are closed in the track list, they are closed in the Mixer. If you like that default behavior, that's fine. If you prefer, though, to have the stacks displayed independently in the Mixer from the Track List, it's easy to change it. In the following screenshot, you can see that under the Mixer's **View** menu, **Follow Track Stacks** is checked:

Figure 13.6 – Follow Track Stacks

Uncheck it. That's it. And if you click in the Mixer to let Logic know that it is now the window that has what they call **Key Focus**, you can now toggle the track stacks open and closed in the Mixer.

Logic Pro X's Mixer is very versatile, with three different views, two of which allow you to filter in/out what you wish to see.

MIXER VIEWS

You can either view the Mixer as part of the integrated main window by simply pressing **X** on your computer keyboard, or as a standalone window by going under the **Window** menu and selecting it, or by pressing **Command + 2** on your keyboard. For now, let's go with the integrated Mixer.

TRACKS VIEW

This is the default view. It is ordered following the Tracks List order. Across the top on the right are tabs that allow you to choose what you want to see displayed at any given time and what you do not. Here, you can see mine with **Master/VCA** and **MIDI** filtered out, and without following **Track Stacks** but with the **Drums** Folder Stack open:

Figure 13.7 – Tracks view in the Mixer

NOTE
A long-standing request by users to the developers is the ability to reorder tracks directly in the Mixer, disregarding their order in the Track List. Maybe sometime in the future, maybe even by the time this book is in your hands, this will be possible, but at the time of writing, sorry, but it's not possible.

SINGLE VIEW

Single view shows you the entire signal path of the channel strip, including any buses that it is sending to for FX plugins. It can be very helpful when you are soloing drums, for instance, to balance the kit. It does not allow you to filter in or out anything because that is not its purpose:

Figure 13.8 – Single view in the Mixer

ALL VIEW

All view shows you all the channel strips that are in your project in the **Environment**:

Figure 13.9 – All view in the Mixer

Whaaaatttt? Environment? What's the Environment?

THE ENVIRONMENT – A BRIEF OVERVIEW

For many, many years, if you were learning about Logic Pro, you would have had to learn about how to use the **Environment**. For some users, it was a scary area that was difficult to understand. For those of us who like to get under the hood and understand it, it was a magical area where you could do things you couldn't really do in other DAWs.

As a beginner, you will never need to go there. But if you press **Command + 0** on your computer keyboard, it opens up, and you can see that there are layers, and that you can create and delete layers:

Figure 13.10 – The Environment

Every channel strip in your project resides as an **object** in the **Environment**, whether you see it in the track list or not. Think of it this way, perhaps: the **Environment** is your closet, where you keep all your clothing. The track list is a suitcase you pack to take on a trip.

If you delete a channel strip from the **Environment**, it will not be available in the track list because, continuing with our analogy, you threw that pair of pants out!

But is the opposite true? That depends on a project setting whose name does not really tip off what it does:

1. Go to **File | Project Settings | Audio**.

2. Select the **Channel Strips** tab.

3. Notice that **Automatic management of channel strip objects** is checked by default:

Figure 13.11 – Automatic management of channel strip objects

If you leave it checked, when you delete a track from the track list, it will also delete the object in the **Environment**. If you uncheck it, it won't. You probably want to leave it checked, except possibly in a template where you may want things to remain in your **Environment** that you don't have in your track list, in case while working you decide you need them.

As I said, Logic has evolved to a point where you, as a beginner, need not ever have to deal with the **Environment**.

CREATING CUSTOMIZED SCREENSETS

Screensets are an awesome feature of Logic Pro. They allow easy recall with a keystroke to create combinations of windows and editors, resized and zoomed in the way you want them, with the tool assignment and with **Snap** and **Drag** assignments. It's the only way, for instance, that you can see both the **Piano Roll** and **Score** editors in the same window.

For our purpose in this chapter, we will explore using them to combine Mixer views. The more screen real estate you have with your monitor(s), the more advantageous they can be.

CREATING A LOCKED CUSTOM SCREENSET

Let's begin by pressing the number **2** on your computer keyboard. By default, it opens a main window. If you click on the **Close** button at the top-left corner of the window, you will quickly discover that Logic thinks you want to close the project, which you don't. So, before you can close this window in the Screenset, you need to add another. If you want the Main Window to remain in the Screenset, you can minimize it:

1. Press **I** on your computer keyboard to hide the Inspector.

2. Go to the **View** menu and choose **Hide Control bar**.

3. Grab the lower right-hand corner of the window and drag it up and to the left to make it as small as possible.

My Screenset 2 now looks as in the following screenshot:

Figure 13.12 – A minimized Main Window in Screenset 2

You are now ready to add a standalone Mixer. Press **Command + 2** on your computer keyboard to open a standalone Mixer. Now you need to decide what you want to see in this Mixer and resize it accordingly if you plan to add a second Mixer. Since many of you are working on a laptop with a single screen, I will assume you just want the one to show you only the audio tracks:

1. Press the tabs at the upper right to filter out everything but **Audio**.

2. Turn off **Follow Track Stacks**, if that is what you want.

3. Position the Mixer on the screen so that it looks the way you want:

Figure 13.13 – A minimized Main Window and Mixer in Screenset 2

After this is done, you will want to lock the Screenset so that you can always return to this view by pressing the number **2**. Scroll up to the Screenset number at the top and choose **Lock**:

Figure 13.14 – Locking a Screenset

Now, if you open plugins, zoom in or out, change Screensets, or make any other changes, you can return to this view by pressing the number **2**.

If you scroll back up to the number **2**, you will find an option to rename the Screenset, if you choose.

DUPLICATING A CUSTOM SCREENSET TO CREATE ANOTHER

If you are happy with the one you created but want another that is almost the same but with a different Mixer view, you don't need to start from scratch:

1. Scroll back up to the number **2**, and you will find an option to duplicate the Screenset.

2. You will then see a dialog box that asks which Screenset number you want to copy it to, and it gives you the opportunity to name it, if you like

Figure 13.15 – Duplicating a Screenset

It looks, as you would expect, exactly like the Screenset you duplicated, but it is unlocked. Let's alter this one by filtering out the audio in the Mixer and filtering in the aux and the output, and then lock the Screenset:

Figure 13.16 – A new Screenset created from a duplicate

You can have up to 90 screensets – 1–9, 11–19 (no 10 or 20), and so on. To access 11 or higher, you have to hold down the **Shift** key and click the two numbers.

You can import a Screenset, along with other project settings, by going to **File | Project Settings | Import Project Settings**. Once there, you will be prompted to point Logic toward the project you wish to import the project settings from and then choose which ones you want to import.

This works fine, but it takes a bit of time, so it is better to save a template with your Screensets, in my opinion.

CREATING MARKERS

Markers are a great way to get around a Logic project, and you can resize their length and move them around easily. So, you should save them in your template. But for this book, I will create them in my project. You can create markers in either the **Global Tracks** or the **Marker List** editor. I will do so in the global Marker track.

CREATING MARKERS IN THE MARKER TRACK

Here is my process:

1. Press **Option + G** to bring up the **Global Tracks** configuration window and hide all but Marker.

2. Click the **+** sign at the upper right at bar 10 to create `Marker 1`.

3. I'm going to create another at bar 5, where my verse begins, and another at 22, for my chorus.

4. Double-click or use the **Text** tool to rename `Marker 1` to `Intro`.

5. Rename the second Marker to `Verse`, and the third to `Chorus`.

The **Marker Track** now looks like this:

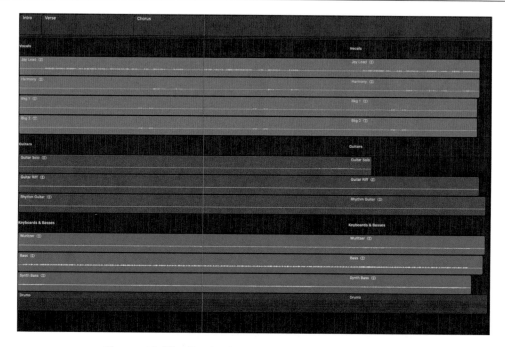

Figure 13.17 – Beginning to create a Marker Track

This doesn't look very inspiring but we will soldier on:

1. Press **Option + C** to open the color palette and give each track a different color so that they pop.

> NOTE
> There is now a Display Preference in the **Tracks** tab to auto-assign colors, but I like to make my own choices.

2. Select the **Verse** Marker and **Option** + drag to copy it to bar 35.

3. Select the **Chorus** Marker and **Option** + drag to copy it to bar 43.

   Now you know how to copy the markers, and we are getting somewhere, but I like clarity. The second verse is only half as long as the first verse, so I want to rename it.

4. Double-click on the second **Verse** Marker and rename it `Verse 2`.

5. Select the **Verse 2** Marker and copy it to bar 56.

6. While the chords are those of the verse, it's a guitar solo, so double-click on this **Verse** Marker and rename it `Guitar Solo`.

7. At bar 64, there is a bridge, so click the **+** sign to create another marker, name it `Bridge`, and color it.

8. Bar 68 is another chorus. Select the **Chorus** Marker and copy it to bar 68.

9. Bar 77 is the outro, and because I like it to be colored the same as the intro, I'll copy the **Intro** Marker and rename it `Outro`:

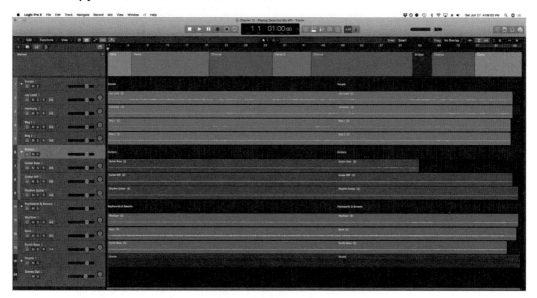

Figure 13.18 – The Marker Track

OK, those look very pretty, but what do I use them for? I am glad you asked!

NAVIGATING YOUR PROJECT WITH MARKER KEY COMMANDS

If you press **Option + K** to open your key commands and in the search file you type the word `Marker`, again you will see that there are a bunch of potentially helpful key commands, but the most important two, for me, are assigned, which are **Go to Previous Marker** and **Go to Next Marker**. I use these so often that I have assigned them to the **F5** and **F6** keys on my computer keyboard:

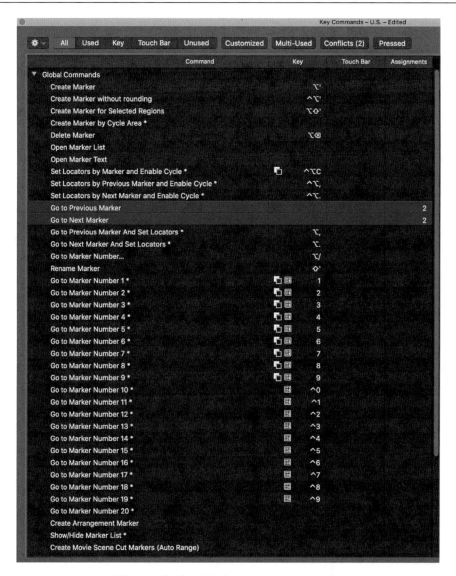

Figure 13.19 – Marker key commands

Now, with the project stopped or playing, I can jump to the next or the previous Marker, which is, as we say where I grew up in Boston, *wicked fast*.

CREATING A CYCLE FROM A MARKER

You can also create a Cycle by dragging a Marker up into the Bar Ruler. If you press **G** on your computer keyboard, it hides the Global tracks, but you see the markers in the Bar Ruler. **Shift** + clicking a Marker in the Bar Ruler creates a Cycle:

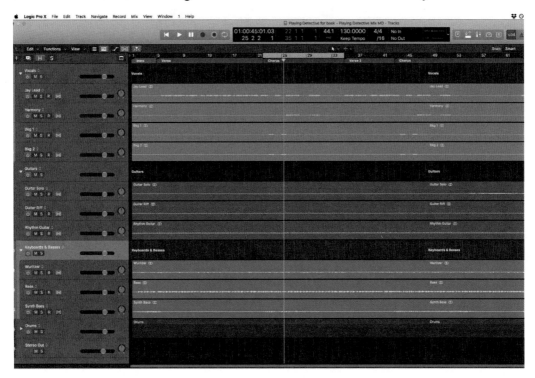

Figure 13.20 – A Cycle created from a Marker in the Bar Ruler

EDITING MARKERS IN THE MARKER LIST

While you can edit markers in the **Marker Track,** I find the **Marker List** easier. Press **D** to open the **List editors** and select the **Marker List**:

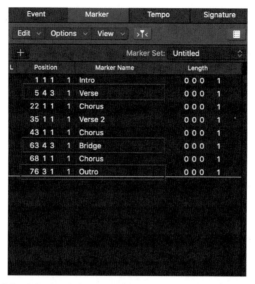

Figure 13.21 – Marker time positions edited in the Marker List

I decided that my markers for the first verse, bridge, and outro should begin a bit earlier to include vocal pickups leading into the sections. All I had to do was drag on the time position to adjust them. So simple.

GIANT BEATS AND GIANT TIME DISPLAY

No matter what size display you have or how many, you may well find that you want to see your bars and beats really large.

On the right side of the LCD, there is a disclosure arrow where you can choose the LCD view, and there you will see the **Open Giant Beats Display** and **Open Giant Time Display** options:

Figure 13.22 – Enabling a Giant display

You have to do them one at a time, which only takes a few seconds. You can then position them on your Screenset, and if it is locked, unlock it, then relock it, and, as our British friends say, *Bob's your uncle*:

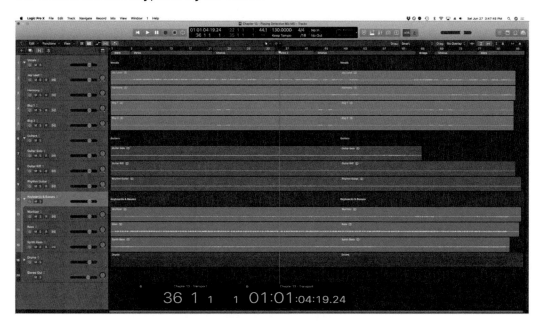

Figure 13.23 – Giant Beats and Giant Time displays

SUMMARY

In this chapter, we covered using **Folder Stacks** for less screen clutter, the three views of the Mixer, and how to best utilize them in custom Screensets. We learned all about markers: creating them, coloring them, and using them to navigate our project and create Cycles. We also learned how to edit them. Finally, we learned how to create giant displays of beats and time.

In the next chapter, we will become familiar with the goals of mixing, discuss considerations, and learn how to use the different categories of plugins to achieve good results.

14 MIXING YOUR PROJECT IN LOGIC PRO X

It has often been said that mixing is as much an art as a science, and I agree. I will not teach you how to mix in this book. No other book will really teach you how to mix either, because it is about training your ears and your mind. What I can do is give you the things you need to consider, and the great tools **Logic Pro X** provides you with to achieve good mixes.

We will discuss the following topics in this chapter:

- The goals of a mix
- Creating prominence and sonic space with volume and panning
- Dynamics plugins, EQ, modulation plugins, and delays and reverb
- Other considerations

THE GOALS OF A MIX

When we do a mix, we should have two goals in mind, and they can seem like they are working at cross purposes, but once you understand why, you will head down the right path:

- Hear every sound in your arrangement.
- Make all the parts into a cohesive whole.

If you have worked hard on your arrangement to get it to a state where every part that exists in it serves a musical purpose, then of course you want to hear each one, but not at the expense of the mix not all sounding like a, well, mix.

With a lot of practice and skill, we can achieve both of these goals.

The methods we will be applying to this are as follows:

- Using volume and panning
- **Effects (FX)** plugins
- Sending to FX hosted on **Auxiliary (aux)** channel strips
- Other considerations

With Logic Pro X 10.5, we got a very nice bonus, a Logic project with the song *Ocean Eyes* recorded by Billie Eilish, written and produced by her brother Finneas O'Connell, and it is a great example of an intelligent mix. Finneas has been using Logic Pro since he was 12 years old, back in 2010. I flat out love it.

You will find it if you open **Logic Pro** and choose **New** from **Template**. Once there, you will see a folder called **Demo Projects**, and within it, you will see the **Ocean Eyes** project, which you should choose:

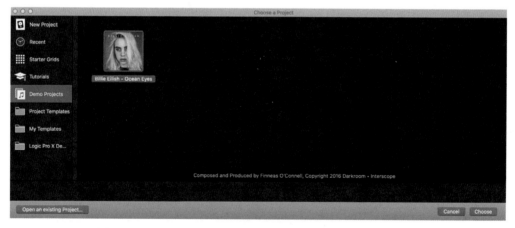

Figure 14.1 – Ocean Eyes in the Demo Projects folder

NOTE
I recommend that once it is loaded, you immediately save a copy so that you don't run the risk of saving over it with changes. Then, close this project and open the copy.

If you are mixing your own song, you will have heard it now tons of times and will be very familiar with it, but unless you have already listened to this *Ocean Eyes* recording a bunch of times, do so now so that you are very familiar with it.

Press **X** to open the Mixer and you will see the software instruments and FX plugins that were employed:

Figure 14.2 – Ocean Eyes in the Mixer

VOLUME

It's pretty obvious that the most important elements of this recording are the vocals and, at the beginning, the Drum Machine Designer parts, and sure enough, just looking at the faders shows you that they are indeed being employed at a greater volume than the other parts. There are some changes in the vocal levels over the course of the songs that are accomplished with automation, which we will discuss in *Chapter 15, Automating Your Mix*, but not a lot. Because of the dreamy nature of the song, not a lot was necessary.

PANNING

If you grew up or presently live in a city where you take the subway, you know that at rush hour, when the car doors open up, it can be really difficult to find a seat or even a place to stand holding a pole. If you get on later in the day, it is far easier as it is less crowded.

The same is true with your mix. If everything is mixed right up in the center, it can be difficult to distinguish the parts. Placing the tracks at different positions in the stereo field is called **panning**, derived from the term *panorama*. So, to create sonic space for every track, you want to have some come up in the center, others maybe slightly to the left, with others more drastically to the left, and others maybe slightly to the right, with others more drastically to the right.

Sure enough, if you open the **Track Stacks** in the Mixer and look at all the vocals, you can see that they have done precisely that, and if you solo them and listen, you will hear how wide it sounds and how every vocal part is clearly distinguishable in the mix:

Figure 14.3 – Panned vocals in the Mixer

There are not a lot of instruments in this production, and the ones that are there are trying to achieve this dreamy kind of wash, so not a lot of panning was necessary. However, one instrument is panned hard left and another hard right, to place them alone in a part of the stereo field:

Figure 14.4 – Panned instruments in the Mixer

Here is a picture of the Mixer in one of my songs, with a busier arrangement than *Ocean Eyes*, and the panning I employed:

Figure 14.5 – Panned instruments in the Mixer in a busier arrangement

BALANCE VERSUS PANNING

Balance is different than panning. Balance knobs control the volume on the left and right signals. If you own a home stereo, it has a balance knob. As you turn it from left to right or right to left while listening to a stereo recording, any material that was panned to one side starts to disappear. You aren't moving anything, just raising and lowering levels on each side.

With true stereo panning, it moves the signal's position in the field, so you move some of the signals to the left or right, while also having the ability to control its width.

On a mono audio track, the balance is just fine and serves as stereo panning because there is not different material on the left and the right. On a stereo audio file, there usually is, and so you may well want to use stereo panning rather than balance.

For years, there was an issue with Logic's pan knob that drove engineers who were more familiar with Pro Tools than Logic Pro crazy. On a stereo audio track, the pan knob was a balance control, so you could not do true stereo panning with it. If you needed or wanted to, you had to open a plugin from the **Imaging** folder called **Direction Mixer**. Now, you no longer have to because it is switchable.

In *Ocean Eyes*, there are only mono audio tracks, as is indicated by the fact that you see one circle instead of two on the **Channel Strip Input** field. If you **Control** + click the **Pan** knob on one of the mono channel strips, you will see that it defaults to **Balance**:

Figure 14.6 – Balance control with the Pan knob on a mono audio track

For this song, therefore, it was a non-issue. But if you have a stereo audio track in your song, you may want to change it to stereo panning and adjust the position and width.

Control + click the **Pan** knob and select **Stereo Pan**, and now it looks like this:

Figure 14.7 – Stereo Pan with the Pan knob on a stereo audio track

For stereo panning:

1. Drag the knob from left to right, then right to left, and you will see that you are moving it around the stereo field, and if you are listening to a stereo file, you will notice that it moves, but does not disappear from the other side as you do.

2. Grab the little white dots on either end of the green slider and you can widen or narrow the signal.

3. You can then grab in the middle of the field you set, and move the left and right positions together, maintaining the same relative panning, but placing the points at different positions in the stereo field.

That's stereo panning, and on a stereo audio track, it is almost always the mode that gives you the control you want:

Figure 14.8 – Stereo panning performed

WORKING WITH FX PLUGINS

There are lots of great FX plugins on the marketplace that either emulate hardware or are unique to software. **Logic Pro X**, however, comes with a really good suite of them, and *Ocean Eyes* is proof of this, in my opinion. So, before you reach for your credit card, spend time with Logic Pro X's plugins.

> NOTE
>
> I own many third-party plugins, so the screenshots you see in this chapter will not be exactly what you see if you only have the Logic Pro-included FX plug-ins.

PLUGIN CATEGORIES

The **Dynamics processor** plugins control level. **Compressor**, **Limiter**, and **Noise Gate** are three examples of these that we will discuss:

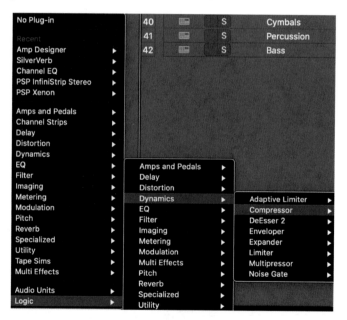

Figure 14.9 – Dynamics plugins

EQ plugins, short for **Equalizers**, adjust frequencies throughout the frequency range. They are primarily a problem-solving tool, meant to either boost or attenuate (lower) certain frequencies that either cause problems within the track or between tracks:

Figure 14.10 – EQ plugins

Modulation plugins spread the sound for effect. **Chorus**, **Tremolo**, **Phaser**, **Flanger**, and **Rotor Cabinet** (Leslie speakers) are all examples of these:

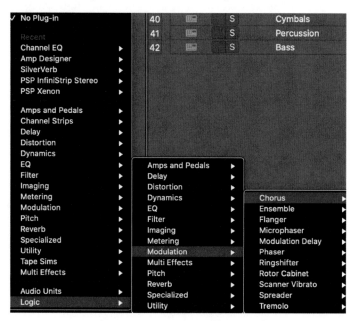

Figure 14.11 – Modulation plugins

Delay plugins do precisely that; they delay sending the signal for a time, creating repeating and rhythmic or arrhythmic effects:

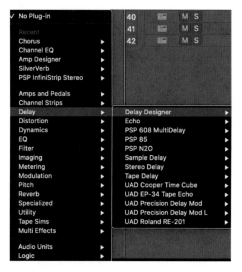

Figure 14.12 – Delay plugins

Reverb plugins place tracks in an ambiance, such as a concert hall, nightclub, church, stairway, and so on. They can range from the barely noticeable to the very lush. Usually, we like to use buses to send from individual channel strips to **Reverb** plugins hosted on auxes, but not always. We will discuss that later in the chapter:

Figure 14.13 – Reverb plugins

Logic Pro X comes with over 70 FX plugins. **Amp Designer** and **Bass Designer** are especially popular with users who do not record their guitars and basses through an amplifier, but we are going to focus on the ones that are used in *Ocean Eyes*.

MANAGING FX PLUGINS

You can add, remove, and bypass plugins in the Mixer, and even copy one or more from one channel strip to another.

Let's go through this together:

1. Create three new mono audio tracks by clicking the + sign at the top of the track list, not record enabled.

2. In the Mixer, select the first one of the three, and on the top empty FX slot, hold the mouse down and add any FX plugin you want:

Figure 14.14 – Adding an FX plugin to a channel strip

I loaded a **Compressor** plugin.

3. In the slot directly below it, add a second FX plugin:

Figure 14.15 – Two FX plugins on a channel strip

4. Hold the mouse down on the plugin in the center click zone of the first slot and drag it to the second audio channel strip to move it (pressing on the left-side click zone will power it off, and clicking on the right-side click zone will open a plugin selection menu).

5. Press **Command + Z** to undo that.

6. While holding down the **Option** key, again, hold the mouse down on the plugin in the first slot and drag it to the second audio channel, and this time you have copied it.

7. Do the same for the plugin on the second slot.

8. To remove the second-copied plugin, hold the mouse down on the right-side click zone of the plugin and choose **No Plug-in**:

Figure 14.16 – Removing an FX plugin on a channel strip

9. On the left-side click zone of the plugin in the plugin slot, you will see a power button. Click on it, and the plugin turns gray and is bypassed.

10. To turn it back on, do it again and it is again active.

11. To do a bunch of them on a channel strip, start at the top power button and drag down. To turn them back on, do it again and they are back.

There is a very helpful unassigned key command that I recommend you assign. It will affect as many or as few channel strips as you select in the Mixer:

Figure 14.17 – The bypass all FX plugins key command

Unfortunately, at the time of writing this, you cannot toggle them on and off; you must press **Command + Z** to undo it. I am fairly confident that by the time that you have this book in your hands, that will no longer be true.

Now that you know how to manage plugins, you can delete the three newly created audio tracks.

PROBLEM-SOLVING WITH EQS

EQs are problem-solving tools. You can use them to attenuate frequencies that are not useful because they are mudding up the sound or boost other frequencies that you think help the track pop in the mix a little more, for example. Engineers generally advise people to listen for frequencies that are bothersome and attenuate them, rather than boosting others that you find lacking, but in fact, they do both. However, they recommend the former because you are less likely to do harm with it. When you boost the frequencies, you run the risk of overloading the next plugin in the chain, such as a compressor, which would then be compressing an EQed sound, and it may not sound good.

There are many different kinds, and Logic has emulations of some vintage EQs, such as a Pultec, an API console EQ, and a Neve Console EQ, and they do sound different; but for learning purposes, we will turn to the one that is reserved for a special thumbnail at the top of the channel strip, Logic's Channel EQ.

THE CHANNEL EQ

The **Channel EQ** is an 8-band Parametric EQ with an Analyzer that is extremely helpful for troubleshooting. By default, bands 1 and 8, low-cut and high-cut filters, are turned off. The low-cut band does just that; it cuts very low frequencies while allowing higher frequencies to *pass* through. You will sometimes see this band referred to as high pass. The high cut, sometimes referred to as low pass, does just the opposite. It cuts very high frequencies and allows lower frequencies to pass through:

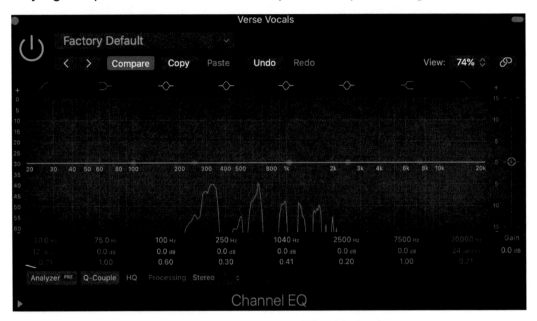

Figure 14.18 – The Channel EQ with Analyzer

Let's use EQ to fix a muddy vocal recording:

1. Go to the **Verse Vocals** track, **track 1**, and set it to **solo**.

2. Bypass all the plugins except the Channel EQ.

3. Click on the **EQ** thumbnail in the Inspector.

4. Turn on the **Analyzer** and click on the word **Post** to change it to **Pre** and start playback. Now, the **Analyzer** is showing you the frequencies in the recording before the **EQ** adjustments you see they have made.

5. While it is still playing, click the power button in the upper left-hand corner to bypass the plugin, and toggle it on and off to hear the difference.

6. Turn the **Analyzer** back to **Post**, or turn it off by clicking on the word **Analyzer**, since it has done its job and consumes some CPU.

    What the **Analyzer** showed us is that this vocal was well recorded. There were not a lot of low frequencies where her vocal range doesn't actually produce sound, so the low-cut filter had little that had to be done. And yet we see that they did in fact do some low cut, boosted some low mids, scooped out a small amount, and then boosted some of the higher frequencies.

7. Turn off **solo** and start playback. Notice that the adjustments in the EQ curve work really well, as her voice has clarity in the mix that it does not have without it.

When you are working on your own tracks, you can grab control points in the EQ and drag them left to right and up and down, and observe, both with your ears and your eyes, how the sound changes. Eventually, you will decide on the frequencies you think you need to attenuate or boost, toggling between soloing and listening in context. It takes a long time and experience to master this, but you want to start trying.

Alternatively, you may well want to start with a preset.

Let's talk a bit about presets. If you ask a professional engineer which EQ they reach for first on a female vocal and which frequencies they generally need to boost or attenuate, the answer will probably be something like "*I don't use presets. Every mix is different.*"

The engineer is telling you the truth, sort of. They may not dial in a preset, but *everyone* has starting points. It is just that the engineer has them in their head or they have created their own plugin presets because they have a lot of mixing experience.

You probably do not, so presets are a great way to get you started. You will modify them as you listen, but they put you in the ballpark. The bottom line is, presets are your friend for educational purposes.

In this screenshot, I have opened up a second **Channel EQ** and loaded the **Brassy Vocal** preset. As you can see, while the two are not identical, they are pretty close, and if you were mixing a singer that sounds like Billie, you could well start there. Maybe Finneas did:

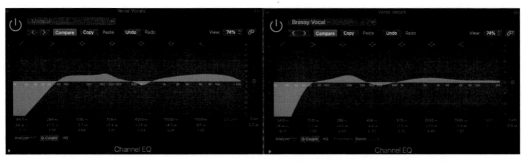

Figure 14.19 – Billie's EQ settings and the Brassy Vocal preset

There is a second **EQ** in the 5th slot, **Vintage Console EQ**. This is an emulation of the EQ in a famous Neve console. They are prized for their warmth and have been used to record and mix lots of hit records that you know and love. As there are three plugins in between the two EQs, it is possible that the second was employed to clean up a little muddiness that they introduced, but my guess is it was just to add a little mojo to the sound, which to my ears, it does.

The vocals are really layered in this mix, with two vocal **Summing Stacks**, named **Vocal Stack** and **Vocal Textures**. If you open them up, you will see that there is a **Channel EQ** with exactly the same settings on every track, which gives it a very homogenized sound. Each **Summing Stack** also has an **EQ** on the stack itself, as do all of the instrument tracks.

I recommend that you spend a lot of time checking out all the EQs so that you can hear how they sound with and without them, and learn which sonic properties they were trying to alter.

CONTROLLING DYNAMICS

If your volume levels vary too much in the range from soft to loud, it can often create problems when you mix, and also affect their prominence in the mix. Logic gives you lots of dynamic processing plugins, and I will explain their differences to you now.

COMPRESSORS

Returning to the second slot on **Verse Vocals**, we find **Compressor**:

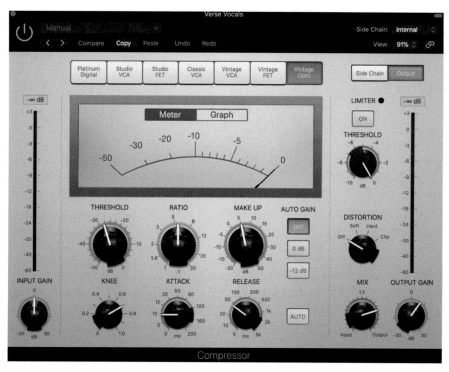

Figure 14.20 – The Logic compressor

A **compressor** does just that; it compresses the signal so that there is less dynamic range, making it more consistent. A **compressor**, therefore, frequently can be another problem-solving tool for when the singer has not been consistent with their volume level, either because of poor mic technique or just the nature of the song. It evens the level out by reducing the loudest parts.

In the hardware world, there are lots of different kinds of compressors with different properties. Some of the most famous are the Teletronix LA-2A optical compressor; DBA 160 VCA (voltage-controlled amplifier); Universal Audio 1176 FET (filed effect transistor); among others.

The Logic compressor gives you two flavors of each, vintage and modern, in addition to its own, **Platinum Digital**. The truth is, in the hardware world, the differences are more obvious, but if you scroll through the different models by pressing the radio buttons at the top center of the interface while playing back, you will hear some differences.

The key settings are as follows:

- **Threshold**: How loud the signal must be before the compressor kicks in
- **Attack** and **Release**: How fast it kicks in and how quickly it releases
- **Ratio**: How squashed the compressed sound gets with the compressed signal
- **Knee**: How the compressors transition between non-compressed and compressed signal, usually *soft* or *hard*

Mix and **Output** affect how loud the compressed signal is versus the non-compressed signal and how loud the compressor outputs, respectively, while the makeup gain allows you to adjust the compressor so that whether it is in or out, the volume doesn't change.

If you look at pictures of the *real thing*, you will see that some of them don't have all those knobs that you see in the Logic version.

But Logic Pro's **Compressor** is not only a problem-solver; it's a creative tool. If you solo the **Verse Vocals** track and bypass the compressor while looking at the fader, you will see that Billie did not sing with a wide dynamic range; she was pretty controlled and sang somewhat softly. When you turn it on, though, even though **Threshold** is set so low that it visually looks like it is hardly getting engaged, the sound is not only louder, it's more in your face, almost equivalent to someone walking toward a video camera and moving their face closer to the lens. It gives the track more presence and prominence in the mix, even at a lesser volume. This effect is heightened in this track by **Output Gain** and **Mix** being cranked up past their default setting. On this track, it makes a huge difference.

Compression is a big factor in almost every contemporary production, and here you see a compressor on almost every track, as well as on the stereo output. When things are louder, we think they sound better, and in this era, music is very compressed.

As I don't want to be the guy yelling "*You kids get off my lawn!*", I will say no more.

LIMITERS

Limiter is similar to **Compressor**, but essentially, it controls signal by drawing a line in the sand and saying *thou shalt go no further*. It prevents tracks from going into the red and potentially distorting. There will almost always be a limiter on the stereo output to prevent it from distorting, because as we know, the stereo output is the one channel strip that should never go into the red in a 32-bit float DAW such as Logic Pro. You might want to use it on a track when you want to control the level but don't want the sound to be more in your face.

Logic Pro has its basic limiter and also **Adaptive Limiter**, which rounds and smooths peaks as well as not letting the signal get too loud, and it can be quite lovely, particularly on the stereo output after a compressor, which is how it is used here:

Figure 14.21 – Adaptive Limiter

NOISE GATES

Finally, we arrive at **Noise Gate**, which in this production is used on almost all the vocal tracks:

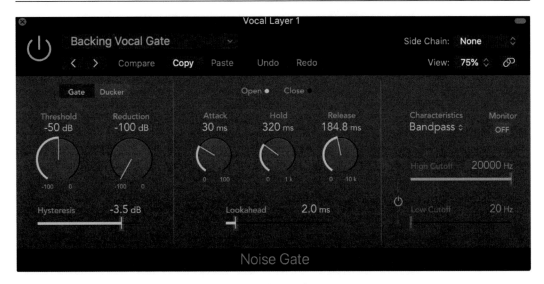

Figure 14.22 – Noise Gate

A noise gate's job is to suppress unwanted audible noise, hum, and cross-talk from other sources that can be heard in the silences when the level is quite low. All these background vocals were indeed sung very softly:

1. Create a Cycle for the chorus by **Shift** + clicking the **Chorus** marker in the bar ruler.

2. Choose **Track 12**, **Vocal Layer 1**, and open the **Noise Gate** plugin. Notice that this is in fact a stock **Logic Noise Gate** preset, called **Backing Vocal Gate**.

3. Start playback and you will see that the gate shifts from **Open** to **Close**, as needed. Much like in the **Compressor**, **Threshold** plays a key role here.

Getting rid of the unwanted noise, especially in a very transparent song such as this, makes for a much cleaner mix.

MODULATION PLUGINS

Modulation plugins are a category that includes effects that can add motion, width, or depth to the sound, slightly delaying the signal by milliseconds, and using **Low-Frequency Oscillation (LFO)** to modulate the signal or amount of delay. Logic has a good amount of them:

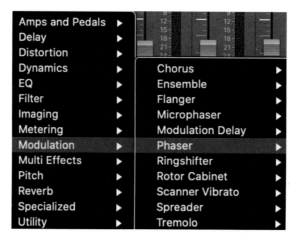

Figure 14.23 – Modulation plugins

They have been used in pop/rock music on almost every instrument, and even on vocals. They have the opposite effect of **Compressor** in that they make the track seem to sit back in the mix a bit at the same volume.

For this song, at least, they were not used very much. In fact, the only one I see is an **Ensemble** plugin on **Track 29**. But we can get creative here:

1. **Shift** + select tracks 24–29, press **Command + D**, and create a **Summing Stack**.

2. Solo it and **Shift** + click the **Chorus** Marker in the Bar Ruler to create a Cycle.

3. Add a Chorus, Phaser, Rotor Cabinet, Tremolo, and a Flanger to the **Summing Stack**, and with all of them bypassed while playing back, listen to each pass through the chorus with one of them made active.

You will probably find the sounds familiar and think of recordings where you have heard the sound of this kind of **Modulation** effect.

DELAYS

Delay is an audio effect that plays back an audio sample again and again after a period of time. It can sync with the project tempo or not. There are five kinds included with Logic Pro, ranging from a simple echo to the very complex and amazing **Delay Designer**.

Delay Designer is a *multitap* delay, meaning that it can create up to 26 steps of delay in a single instance, creating some really wild effects. You probably would only turn to it, however, in EDM or **ambient** music, so it bears no relationship to this song. But if you are into creating music in those genres, you will want to spend more time with it:

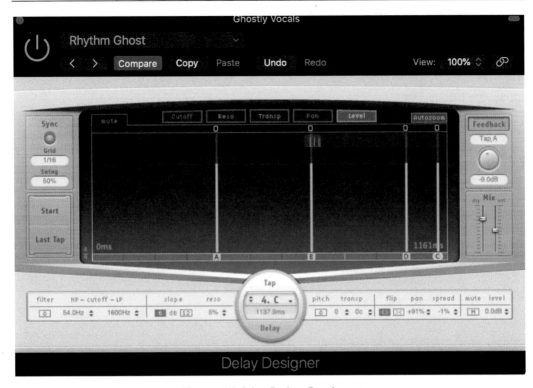

Figure 14.24 – Delay Designer

The **Echo** plugin is just that, a simple echo, and sometimes it is all you need:

Figure 14.25 – The Echo delay

Sample Delay is an outlier here, as it is less of an effect than a utility, as it can be set to delay a channel by single sample amounts. In all candor, I have never used it:

Figure 14.26 – Sample Delay

The two you most commonly will use are **Tape Delay** and **Stereo Delay**.

If you have heard the sound of early Rockabilly records from the '50s and '60s by Elvis Presley, Gene Vincent, and others, you are already very familiar with the sound of a tape delay, which was produced with tape recorders by shortening or lengthening a loop of recording tape and adjusting the read and write heads:

Figure 14.27 – Tape Delay

It is a very warm sound and still beloved by recording artists. John Lennon of *The Beatles* loved tape delay and used it on most of his vocals.

Generally, you will want not to sync it to tempo, but dial in your own rates, and adjust the dry and wet faders to your liking. More feedback means more repeats. I often use a setting such as what you see in the preceding screenshot on my own vocals.

Stereo Delay is the one used in this production, again on a ton of tracks. It is a software version of a digital delay, such as the iconic Lexicons and TC Electronic delays, and is perhaps the most versatile:

Figure 14.28 – Stereo Delay

Here, you can see the settings on the lead vocal, and as you can see, it is tempo-synced with very little output, which makes it quite subtle:

1. Solo the track and bypass it, and then make it active, repeatedly; you will hear that it adds some depth to the sound and is really lovely.

2. Solo all the vocals and play back the chorus, and again you will hear a lovely sort of homogenized sound.

If you open multiple **Stereo Delay** instances from the tracks, you will see that they have identical settings, which leads to that homogenized effect.

REVERBS

What is reverb? If you walk into a big church with high ceilings and clap your hands loudly, what you hear reflected back is **reverb**. When you walk into a stairwell and do the same, that is also reverb. A **Reverb** plugins are an ambiance generator and can be used to place the sound as if it were in a concert hall, night club, scoring stage, or outdoor venue, among others.

Early reverberation was created with echo chambers, plates, springs, and other mechanical devices and are still used today. Later, there were digital reverbs by

Lexicon, Eventide, and others that used mathematical algorithms to recreate those ambiances and the aforementioned venue types.

With plugins, there are essentially two types:

- **Algorithmic:** Generally speaking, algorithmic reverbs are more of an effect rather than an accurate recreation of a specific location. They are prized for their ability to add sheen and gloss to a sound, as well as some special chorusing that some, such as the famous Lexicons, add.
- **Convolution:** Convolution reverbs use samples, in **Impulse Responses (IRs)**. People who create IRs go to the venues and record the ambiance with microphones. So, a well-recorded IR will be a more accurate recreation of a specific venue rather than an algorithmic reverb.

Logic comes with three of the former and one of the latter. **Enverb** and **SilverVerb** are older Logic algorithmic reverbs. I rarely see **Enverb** used much anymore, but **SilverVerb** still gets used a lot on percussion and drums, because it is simple, sounds great on short sounds, and is very light on the CPU. It is generally used directly on a channel strip, as it is in this song on three channel strips:

Figure 14.29 – SilverVerb

Logic Pro's newest algorithmic reverb is called **ChromaVerb**, and I think it sounds great. It gives you a lot of control over its pre-delay before it kicks in, as well as size, density, and other settings, and it has a built-in EQ for taking out any perceived muddiness. It also has that gloss and sheen when you need it. Apparently, though, in this project, it was not the reverb of choice:

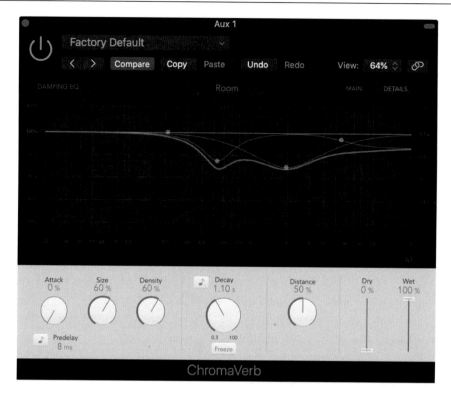

Figure 14.30 – ChromaVerb

Logic Pro's convolution reverb is called **Space Designer**, and it also sounds great, with tremendous control:

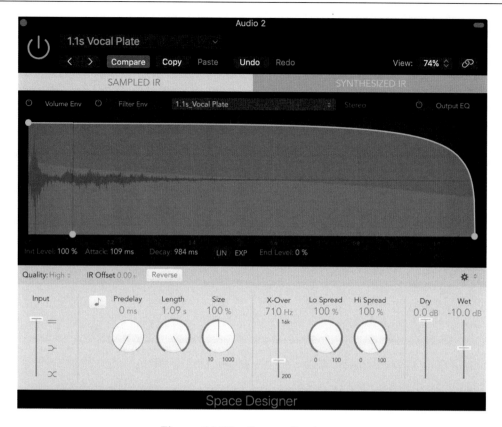

Figure 14.31 – Space Designer

There are five of them used in this project, all instantiated on auxes, all assigned to buses that send to them, as is done with hardware units plugged into recording consoles.

In the hardware world, the reasons to bus to them were obvious. The great ones were/are darned expensive, so there were only so many you had available. In the software world, we mostly do it to save CPU, resources but also, it gives you a more subtle level of control than when they are opened directly on a channel strip. Frequently, you also want to give the impression that the performers were in the same place or places, although not always.

Logic makes the creation of auxes with buses super easy. Let's see how it is done.

Open the `Chapter 14` **Logic project:**

Figure 14.32 – A little project with vocals

Here, I have four vocal tracks that I want to send to two reverbs, **ChromaVerb** and **Space Designer**, for a hybrid reverb effect:

1. **Shift** + select the four tracks and hold down on **Send**, and select an unused bus.

    As you can see in the following screenshot, Logic automatically created an aux with that chosen bus as its input:

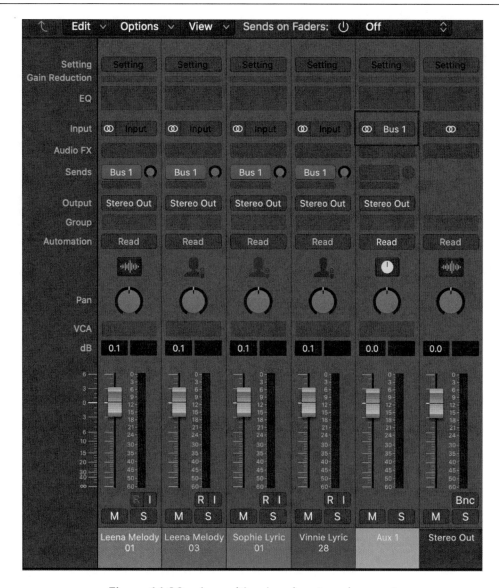

Figure 14.33 – Aux with a bus input assignment

2. Repeat the process and another aux is created with the correct bus input.

3. Instantiate a **ChromaVerb** reverb with a preset on **Aux 1**, and a **Space Designer** reverb with a preset on **Aux 2**.

4. Press play and listen to that gorgeous reverb:

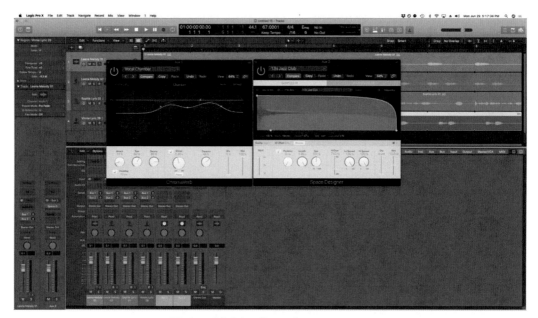

Figure 14.34 – Reverbs on auxes

You don't hear it? No, you don't, because you control the amount you hear by sending from the tracks.

5. With all the vocal channel strips in the Mixer selected, press play and turn the **Bus 1** send knob slowly to the right, and now you will start to hear the **ChromaVerb** reverb.

6. With all the vocal channel strips in the Mixer selected, press play and turn the **Bus 2** send knob slowly to the right, and now you start to hear the **Space Designer** reverb.

7. Clicking on the power button on either to bypass it allows you to hear one or the other in isolation:

Figure 14.35 – Reverbs on auxes receiving a level from sends

MIXING AS YOU GO VERSUS STARTING FROM SCRATCH

Here is where we come to a very subjective topic. I will give you my views, but others will disagree, and they are not necessarily right or wrong.

I started at a time when the common practice was for an engineer to set levels for players while they were tracking their parts, and then when it came time to mix, the engineer would pull all the faders down and start from scratch, by balancing and panning the drums, or maybe the vocals.

People working with samples and software instruments mostly mix as they go, and I do too.

When time permits, however, I prefer to do the following:

- Create a new Project Alternative.
- Bounce and replace all my software instrument tracks so that now I am only dealing with audio.
- Pull down the faders and start from scratch.

Why do I prefer doing this? Well, because I am a composer who learned to mix, rather than an engineer who learned to compose, I think differently. This way, I am no longer worrying about the MIDI performances or choices; I am solely focused on making the parts work together. Also, software instruments can sometimes get finicky, especially resource-demanding third-party ones, and their performance can be erratic. They also put more burden on your CPU, which audio does not.

In the end, though, you will eventually discover what works best for you and decide.

I also like to turn on **Pre Fader Metering**. Here is how you do so:

1. Customize your control bar and make sure that **Pre Fader Metering** is checked in the **Modes and Functions** section, and click **OK**:

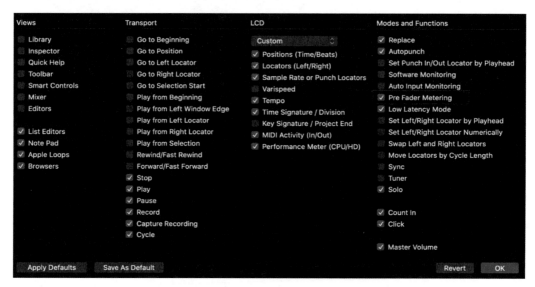

Figure 14.36 – Pre Fader Metering selected

2. Click the **Pre Fader Metering** button to turn it on:

Figure 14.37 – Pre Fader Metering engaged

What happens with pre-fader metering is that as you adjust the volume up or down on your channel strip, even though you hear the sound louder or softer, the level you see displayed on the channel strip does not change. It shows you the amount of signal that the channel strip is receiving. When you have multiple plugins flowing from one into another, sometimes if one is outputting a hot signal, the one following it does not handle it well and the sound, while not actually digitally distorting, may not sound good. This is especially true when you start using third-party FX. So, if something sounds off, while it may not be the channel strip that is going wildly into the red, it's as good a place to start troubleshooting as any.

The other advantage is that we should be mixing with our ears more than our eyes. I like to turn a fader all the way down, then gradually raise the level, sometimes with my eyes closed, until it sounds right to me.

Some users I know never use pre-fader, only post-fader. Others only use pre-fader. Most engineers that I know go back and forth between the two, at different stages of the mix.

OTHER CONSIDERATIONS

Here are some final thoughts I will share with you about mixing. As promised, I did not teach you to mix because I can't. It takes a lot of practice.

A mix will always sound somewhat different on different playback systems, but the intention is to create one that sounds good on as many as is possible, which is often referred to as how a mix *translates*.

The following factors will affect your ability to create a mix that you know will sound good on other systems:

- Your room.
- Your studio monitors (speakers, not computer displays).
- Your other playback options.

If you do not have a room that has been acoustically treated, and most of us don't, bass frequencies can get trapped, so you don't get an accurate bass level for translation. There are a number of solutions:

- Buy some acoustic panels and set them up. There are a lot of tutorials on how to do this on the internet.

- Buy room correction software that is designed to help with this. There are several and opinions vary wildly as to how well they work.

- Buy studio monitors with built-in room correction software that is designed to help with this. Again, there is some disagreement, but I think that some companies get it right. There are lots of reviews online.

- Put up bookcases, staggering different-sized books, so that the frequencies are less likely to get trapped.

At the end of the day, though, it will come down to how well you know how your monitors help you translate in your specific room. In my case, because I have a three-way speaker system with a subwoofer in an untreated room, I know that if I find myself wanting just a little more bass, it will translate well, whereas if the bass is exactly at the level I like, it will be a bit bass-heavy on other systems.

I recommend that you listen to your mix on as many different playback systems as possible. I listen through headphones, burn the mix onto a CD, and play it back on a boombox and in the CD player in my car.

I also suggest you bring commercial mixes of projects that are in a similar genre and compare it to your mix; although they will be mastered, so yours will not sound as loud or as good. We will discuss mastering in *Chapter 16*, *Delivering Your Music for Distribution*.

When you are mixing, listen at different volumes. Mixing only at full volume can make you think your mix sounds better than it does. Take frequent breaks to prevent your ears from having mix fatigue.

Obviously, if you can sit in on a mixing session with an experienced engineer and listen and observe what they do, it can be very informative.

There are lots of videos about mixing available online, some paid, some free, some with very famous engineers. They too can be helpful, but keep in mind that they are usually created to either generate income for the engineer or to encourage you to buy third-party plugins.

It will take a fair amount of time and practice to be able to achieve a good mix, but it is a realistic goal for you.

SUMMARY

In this chapter, we covered the goals of a mix, and how to achieve them using volume, panning, and different kinds of FX plugins. I also gave you some advice on what to expect from your mixing environment, and how to listen to your finished mix to evaluate it.

In the next chapter, we will become familiar with how to use automation, both offline and with the project playing back, to bring liveliness and movement to your mixes.

15 AUTOMATING YOUR MIX

In *Chapter 14, Mixing Your Project in Logic Pro X*, we focused on mixing, but when it came to setting volume levels, pan positions, and all the settings in the plug-ins, everything we did was what is often referred to as *set and forget*. Sometimes that works just fine, but, more often than not, automating the levels, panning, and plug-ins so that the parameter values change over time can bring a sense of movement and liveliness to your project.

In this chapter, we will discuss the following topics:

- A brief history of automation
- Creating region automation without the project playing
- Creating track automation with the project playing in Touch mode
- Creating track automation with the project playing in Latch mode
- Editing and deleting automation

A BRIEF HISTORY OF AUTOMATION

In the 1970s, the development of recording consoles and tape machines progressed to the point where we could now mix multiple 24-track machines synced together. This meant that the engineer might have many more adjustments to make in real time than he could realistically perform with just two hands, or even two engineers with four hands could.

Console makers such as AMS Neve and SSL rose to fill the void with console automation, allowing the console to memorize the engineer's moves. It is often claimed that Queen's *Bohemian Rhapsody* was one of the first records to employ this ability, and as complex as it is, it certainly had to be at least one of the first.

Initially, the faders and knobs would not be moving as you were hearing the changes, but Rupert Neve created a console in the 70s that introduced *flying faders*, and all of today's DAWs can emulate this, as do even inexpensive hardware controllers from companies such as Mackie and Behringer, among others.

In Logic Pro X, virtually any plug-in or channel strip settings you execute in a project can be automated.

To view **Automation** in a Logic project, you simply need to press **A** on your computer keyboard. By default, Logic will show you a lane with volume automation, because volume is the setting that is most frequently automated.

Here, you can see volume automation in *Ocean Eyes*:

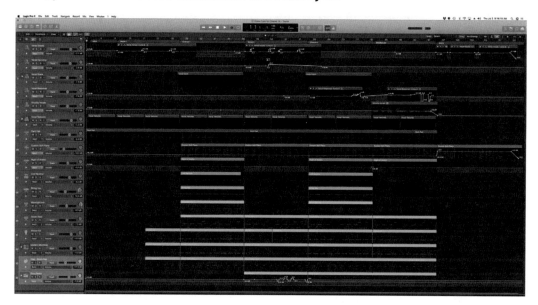

Figure 15.1 – Volume automation in Ocean Eyes

Automation can be achieved both offline, without the project playing, or in real time, with the project playing. Although I can only guess with some of the tracks, track 25 clearly was done offline just by creating a few control points, because there are few movements and they are straight lines. Others could have been performed in real time and edited.

If we click the disclosure triangle, other lanes appear that show additional automation that was performed on this track:

Figure 15.2 – Additional automation in Ocean Eyes

When you play the song back with the Mixer open, you will see the volume moves, as well as hearing some of the plug-in automation, but no panning movement and, overall, not that much automation, because of the dreamy nature of the song.

Tracks and regions can be automated. If you automate a region, then it does not affect other regions that come after in the track. If you copy the region, the automation is copied with it. If you automate a track, then any automation definitely does affect what happens later in that track. We will explore both in this chapter with a new project created entirely from Apple Loops. You may also use Apple Loops for practice or one of your own projects.

Open the Chapter 15 project:

Figure 15.3 – A project created with Apple Loops

OFFLINE REGION AUTOMATION

I am going to begin by automating panning in the region you see on track 8 at bar 3.

REGION PANNING AUTOMATION

Let's begin with the following steps:

1. Press **A** to see automation. It defaults to **Track automation** for volume, the automation is visible on every track, and is assigned to **Read mode**.

2. Should you want this track to be bigger, press **Control + Z** on the computer keyboard or, alternatively, go to the **View** menu and choose **Zoom Focused Track**, and any selected track now gets bigger.

3. Click on the word **Track** and it switches to **Region**, which is what I want to use to create panning for this region in this instance.

4. Hold the mouse down on **Volume** and navigate to **Main | Pan | Absolute**:

Figure 15.4 – Set to create region-based panning automation

As you turn the pan knob from left to right or right to left while listening to a stereo recording, any material that was panned to one side starts to disappear. You aren't moving anything, just raising and lowering levels on each side.

I decide that I would like to begin in the center, pan all the way left, then all the way right, and then return to the center.

5. Click in the **Warp Speed** region at four different horizontal positions, which creates four control points, all set to **0**, center pan:

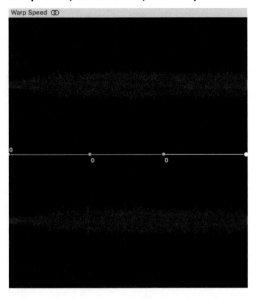

Figure 15.5 – Four control points in the region for pan automation

6. Drag the second control point all the way up to **-64** and the third all the way down to **+63**:

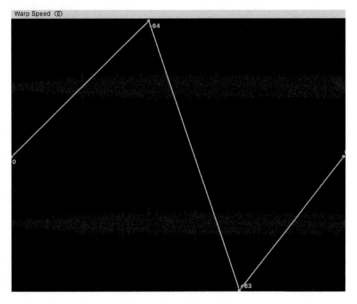

Figure 15.6 – Four control points creating pan automation in the region

7. Press **Control + Z** to turn off **Zoom focused track**.

8. Select the region and, while holding down the **Option** key, drag it to bar 15, making sure you release the mouse before the **Option** key. You will then see that the region is copied with the panning automation, and that there is no automation in between the two regions:

Figure 15.7 – The copied region with the pan automation

Region automation can be converted to **Track automation**, and vice-versa:

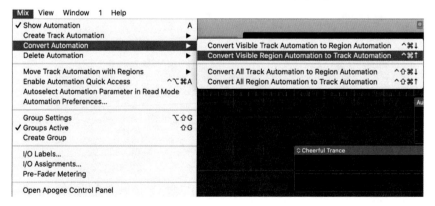

Figure 15.8 – Converting automation from Region to Track

You will then see panning automation before, in between, and after those two regions, but there is no particular advantage to that in this instance.

PLUG-IN BYPASS AUTOMATION IN A REGION

In the **2-Step Remix** region, I have added an **AutoFilter** effect with a preset:

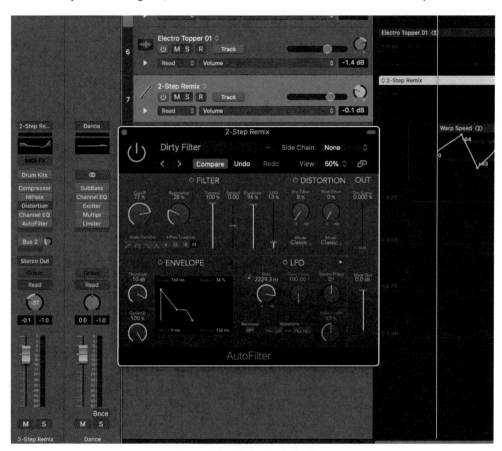

Figure 15.9 – An AutoFilter effect

I want to hear that effect at the beginning, but then bypass it when the **Warp Speed** region enters at bar 3:

1. Change the automation from **Track** automation to **Region** automation, as we did with the panning.

2. Navigate to **Main | Insert 6 Bypass (AutoFilter)**.

   Here is another instance where key commands are your friend.

3. Press **Ctrl + Shift + Command + 2** to create control points at the borders of the region. Excellent!

4. Create another control point at bar 3 and drag it down.

5. Play back from the beginning and you will see and hear the plug-in initially, but not when it is bypassed at bar 3:

Figure 15.10 – An AutoFilter effect with bypass automated in the region

If I copy the region, that automation will be included.

LIVE TRACK AUTOMATION

Clicking in control points without playback is a very precise way to automate, but sometimes you just want the feel of doing this in real time. This is especially true with volume, where listening to a part and riding the fader produces a very musical result.

AUTOMATION MODES

There are four **Automation Modes**, as can be seen here:

Figure 15.11 – The Automation Modes

- **Read**: Reacts to any automation. Turning it off does not remove the automation, but it is ignored until turned back on.

- **Touch**: While playing the project back, it stays at the level you are drawing with your mouse until you release it, and then snaps back to its original level.

- **Latch**: While playing the project back, it stays at the level you are drawing with your mouse until you release it, and then remains at that level until you resume movement.

- **Write**: While playing the project back, it erases all the automation on that track, whether visible or not.

VOLUME AUTOMATION WITH TOUCH MODE

Let's discover exactly how **Touch Mode** works. You don't need to be in *record* to record automation:

1. Change the Automation mode from **Read** to **Touch**.

2. Start playback and grab either the **Volume** slider in **Track Header** or **Channel Strip Fader** in the Inspector or Mixer and start to raise and lower the volume.

3. While playback continues, release the mouse button for a while, and then resume the movements.

4. Change the Automation mode from **Touch** back to **Read**.

In the following screenshot, it is pretty obvious where I stopped moving the mouse, because with **Touch** mode, it snapped back to the original level:

Figure 15.12 – Touch automation

VOLUME AUTOMATION WITH LATCH MODE

Perform the following similar, but nevertheless different, steps:

1. Change the Automation mode from **Read** to **Latch**.

2. Start playback and grab either the **Volume** slider in **Track Header** or **Channel**

Strip Fader in the Inspector or Mixer and start to raise and lower the volume.

3. While playback continues, release the mouse button for a while, and then resume the movements.

4. Change the Automation mode from **Latch** back to **Read**:

Figure 15.13 – Latch automation

In this screenshot, you can see that when I released the mouse button, it remained at the level I was at, at that point, and it did not snap back to the original. When movement resumed, **Latch** also resumed.

AUTOMATIC LANE CREATION WITH EITHER LATCH OR TOUCH MODE

This is an area where Logic's automation shines. I decide that I want the EQ's bands to be automated in Cycle mode. Do I have to choose a lane each time? No, I do not. Logic will do this for me:

1. Choose the **Autumn Haze** region and open **Channel EQ**. Notice that there have not yet been any EQ adjustments.

2. Change the Automation mode from **Read** to **Touch**.

3. Begin playback and, as it cycles, grab different bands in the EQ and adjust them.

As is evident in the following screenshot, when I open the disclosure triangle, Logic did indeed create automation lanes for each EQ band:

Figure 15.14 – EQ band touch automation

TRIMMING AUTOMATION

Logic gives you lots of ways to alter your automation. To delete control points, select one or more points while holding the *Shift* key, and then just press the *Delete* key and they are gone.

We have two choices for trimming the level of volume automation – Trim and Relative, again both offline and in real time.

OFFLINE TRIM

If you hold your mouse down over the **Automation Value** field, you will see the word **Trim** appear:

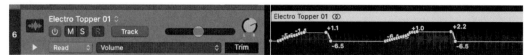

Figure 15.15 – Trim volume

Simply dragging **Trim** up or down makes it lower or higher while preserving all the automation control points.

This isn't limited to volume automation. Remember all those EQ bands that we automated? You can trim the frequency changes in the same manner.

REAL-TIME TRIM

If I return to either **Latch** or **Touch** mode on a track, I now have the option of either choosing **Trim** or **Relative**:

Figure 15.16 – Trim or Relative for Latch or Touch mode

If you choose **Trim**, your Automation mode changes to **T-Latch** or **T-Touch**. If you choose **Relative**, your Automation mode changes to **R-Latch** or **R-Touch**.

With **T-Latch**, a red line begins to appear as I drag down with my mouse:

Figure 15.17 – T- Latch in action

When I stop, the red line disappears, the new values are in place, and the contours are replaced by the new moves.

Coming from the analog world, as I do, I do not think of this as trimming.

With **R-Latch**, a yellow line begins to appear as I drag down with my mouse and when I stop, I see both lines, which indicates that even though it got louder or softer, the original contours are, in fact, preserved:

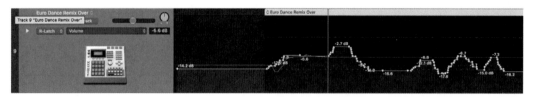

Figure 15.18 – R- Latch results

Personally, I think **Relative** should be called **Trim**, and what is presently called **Trim** should be called **Replace**.

COPYING AUTOMATION

You can copy automation within a track or between tracks, but there are some things you need to understand for the latter.

COPYING AUTOMATION WITHIN A TRACK

Copying visible automation within a track works the same way copying works in the workspace with anything:

1. Select the control points with the **Marquee** tool, or hold down the **Shift** key and drag over them.

2. Hold the mouse down, and they all turn white.

3. While holding down the **Option** key, drag to copy them to the desired location, releasing the mouse first. So easy:

Figure 15.19 – Automation copied within a track

COPYING AUTOMATION BETWEEN TRACKS

The process is slightly different when copying automation between tracks:

1. Select the control points in the track you wish to copy from with the **Marquee** tool or hold the **Shift** key and drag over them.

2. Either go to the **Edit** menu and choose **Copy**, or, better yet, press **Command + C**.

3. Go to the track you wish to copy to, and either go to the **Edit** menu and choose **Paste**, or, better yet, press **command + V**.

THE TRACK AUTOMATION EVENT LIST

Most users do not know about this list, because it is only available by key command. The key command is …. drum roll …. **Ctrl + Command + E**.

It looks pretty much like the **Event List** and works the same way. Here, you can alter existing automation control points to your heart's content:

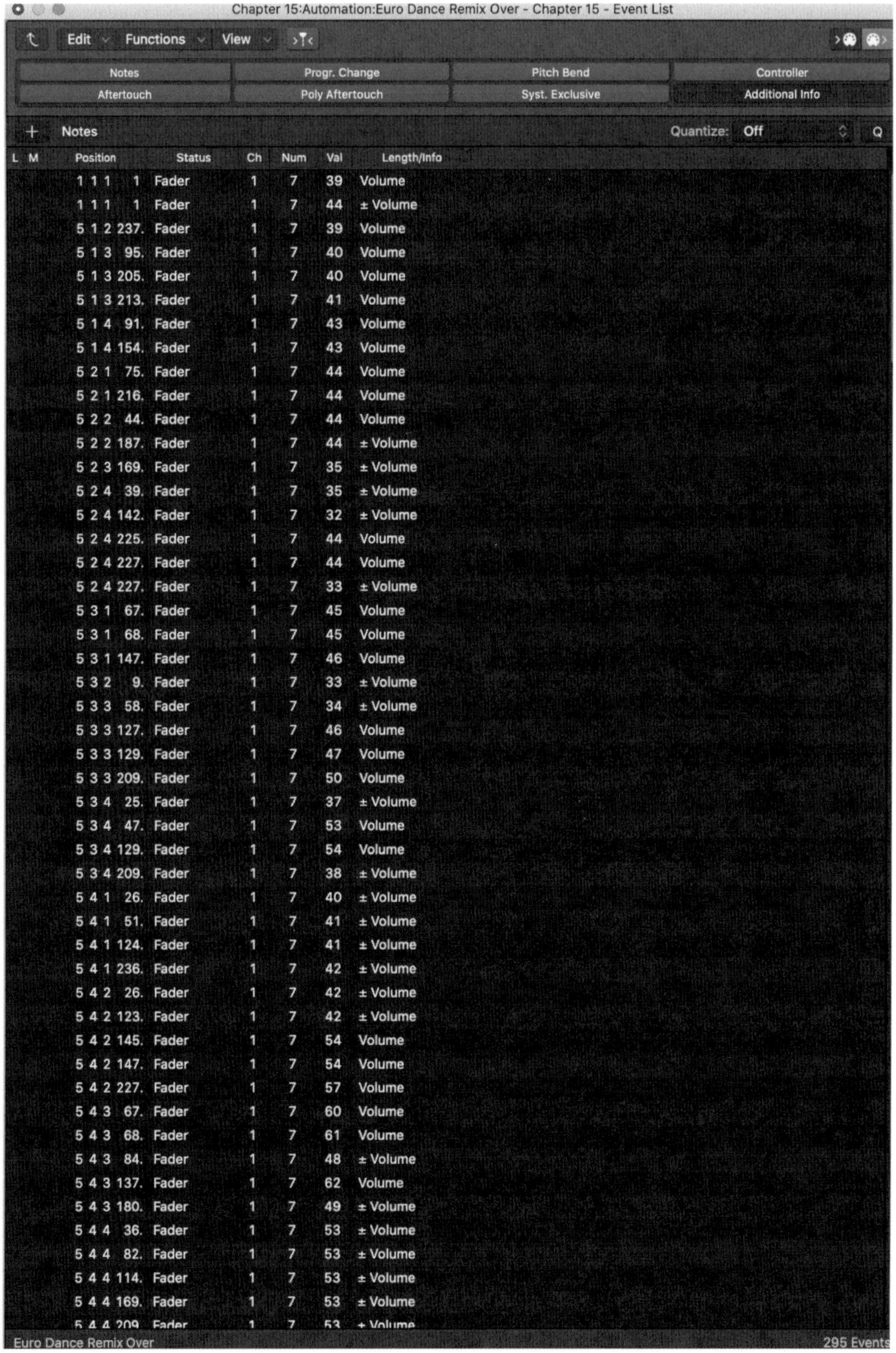

Figure 15.20 – The track automation Event List

The question is, can you select the control points and copy them by pressing **Command + C**, go to another track and open the **Track Automation Event List**, and press **Command + V** to paste them? You betcha!

DELETING AUTOMATION

Automation can easily be deleted by going to the **Mix** menu; with or without being visible on a selected track; all automation on a track; automation on a track where all regions have been deleted, a so-called orphaned track; redundant automation (control) points, or for all tracks as shown in the following screenshot:

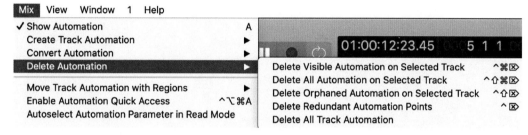

Figure 15.21 – Automation deletion options in the Mix menu

CUSTOMIZING MIDI CONTROLLERS FOR AUTOMATION

If you go to **Mix | Automation Preferences**, the following window appears:

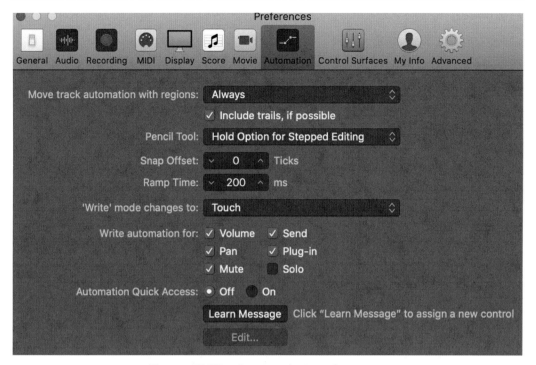

Figure 15.22 – Automation preferences

If I was writing this book a couple of years ago, I would have spent some time instructing you as to how to use Automation Quick Access to teach your MIDI controller to use its knobs or faders to control automation in real time. Nowadays though, there are a slew of affordable MIDI controllers that come with mapping for **Logic Pro X**, so there is no need to do so. If you are a beginner, you should certainly consider buying one.

Alternatively, you can download the free Logic Remote app for an iPad or iPhone if you own one and use that for this purpose.

SUMMARY

In this chapter, we covered a brief history of automation and Logic Pro X's automation capabilities. We learned how to automate both with playback stopped and in real time during playback. We also learned about all the different automation modes for real-time automation, and how to edit, trim, copy, and delete our automation.

In the next chapter, we will become familiar with the concepts of mastering versus pre-mastering, and bouncing a mix or stems for distribution.

16 DELIVERING YOUR MUSIC FOR DISTRIBUTION

Ever notice that commercial recordings sound pretty different from the computer-based productions you have heard from your friends? That is because they go through a process called mastering. Before we get to that, though, we will need to bounce our mix or possibly send our individual tracks to another mix engineer.

We will discuss the following topics in this chapter:

- Bounce options
- Exporting tracks for mixing outside the project
- Mastering and pre-mastering

BOUNCING A STEREO MIX

You have worked really hard on your composition, arranging, and final mix. You are almost ready to send your baby out into the world. Or are you? Perhaps you want to send the individual tracks or combinations of them to another engineer.

Either way, you will first want a stereo mix for yourself, or as a guide to the engineer as to what you are envisioning.

You may consider, if you have not already, whether or not you want a fade out at the end of the track instead of a more abrupt ending. Fade outs can be quite long or quite short, depending on how you want it to sound.

In the following screenshot, you can see that for this song, I automated the stereo output to do a very short fade:

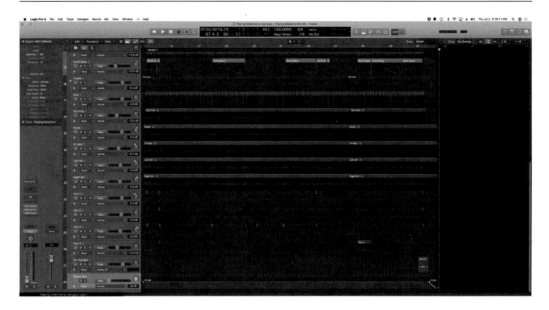

Figure 16.1 – A short automated fade out

The stereo output will be added to the bottom of the track list if you either assign it to an automation mode, or in the Mixer, you select it and go under the **Options** menu and choose **Create Tracks**, or press **Ctrl + T** on your computer keyboard for **Selected Channel Strips**. Once it is there, it will remain at the bottom of the track list. Presently, Logic does not give you the option to move it up in the track list.

Alternatively, go under the **Track** menu and select **Output Track**, or press **Shift + Command + M**.

OPENING THE BOUNCE WINDOW

Again, Logic gives you several ways to get to the window where you will choose your options:

1. Navigate to **File | Bounce | Project** or **Section**.
2. Press **Command + B**.
3. On the **Stereo Output** channel strip, click on **Bnce** (no, that isn't short for Beyoncé).

By now, you know that I am going to use the key command, and when I do, the following window opens up:

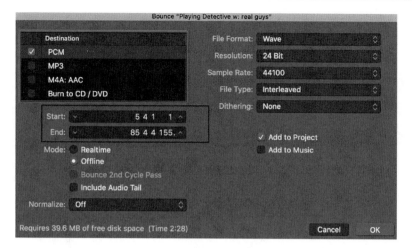

Figure 16.2: The Bounce window with an incorrect bounce length

There is much to learn about in this window, but right away, I see a problem with the length of the bounce. My project is over 80 bars long, but Logic seems to think I only want to bounce a section of it. That is because I had a region selected in the Tracks area when I pressed **Command + B**.

No problem, I deselect the region by clicking in a blank part of the Tracks area and again press **Command + B**. Whaaattt? Now Logic thinks my project is 168 measures long?

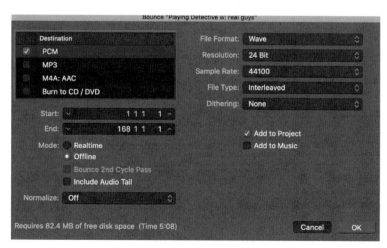

Figure 16.3 – The Bounce window with another incorrect bounce length

There are a couple of ways to prevent this from ever happening. One is to customize your Control bar to include **Key Signature / Project End** under the **LCD** column and make it one of your defaults:

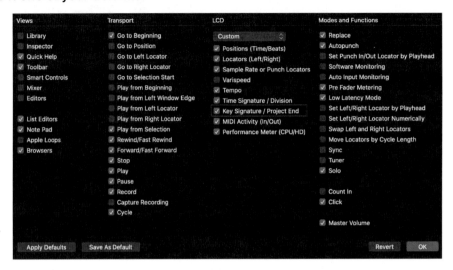

Figure 16.4: Adding Key Signature/Project End to the Control Bar

Now, you can double-click on the number of bars and type in the correct amount – in my case, `88` bars. But there is an easier way:

1. Press **Command** **+ A** to select all the regions.
2. Press **U** to create a Cycle that conforms to the length of all the regions.

Now, when you open the **Bounce** window, it will be correct:

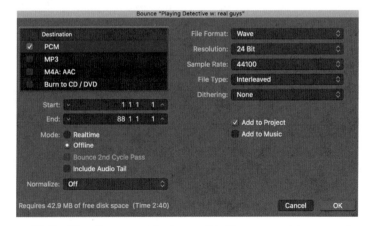

Figure 16.5 – The Bounce window with the correct bounce length

PCM FILE FORMATS

Under the **Destination** menu, the first checkbox is for **PCM**, which stands for **pulse code modulation**. PCMs are high-quality audio files that you use to burn onto a CD or DVD or to give the best quality. If you hold the mouse down on the file format, you see three choices: **AIFF**, **Wave**, and **CAF**:

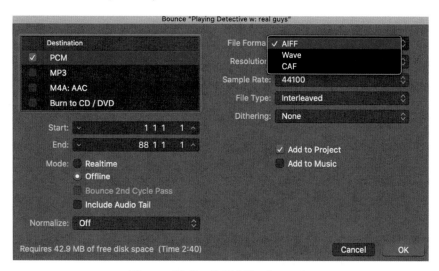

Figure 16.6 – PCM file formats

Many years ago, Macs used Sound Designer II files and PCs used Wave files, and they were not compatible. Apple realized that there were a lot more PC users than Mac users and created the **Audio Interchange File Format**, **AIFF**, a cross-platform format. Eventually, **Wave** files became **Broadcast Wave** files and they too were cross-platform.

So, which should you use? Which one sounds better?

Neither, the sound is the same; they simply write their header information differently. I recommend getting in the habit of using **Wave** because it has become an industry standard.

CAF stands for **Core Audio Format** and was designed for storage, so you can forget about it for our purposes.

If you now examine the **Resolution** field, you have a choice of **8**-, **16**-, **24**-, or **32**-bit float. CDs and DVDs use **16**-bit, but **24**-bit is a lot more resolution, and when you burn it onto a CD or DVD, any app you use to do so will convert it down to 16-bit, so I recommend sticking with that. **32**-bit float is great for when you want to preserve the best quality, but many other programs will not let you import **32**-bit float audio files.

The next field is for the **Sample Rate** selection, which we discussed back in *Chapter 3, Recording Audio*.

There is no sonic improvement in up-sampling from where your project audio was recorded. You cannot add bits that are not there. So, if you recorded at **44.1**, stay at **44.1** unless it is going to DVD or a video editing program, in which case you want to choose **48**.

In the **File Type** field, there are only two choices: **Split** and the default, **Interleaved**. Unless an engineer specifically requests separate left and right sides of a stereo audio file, there is no reason for you not to always choose **Interleaved**.

Now we come to **Dithering**. Dithering is a more complicated subject. Most pros will tell you that when you are going to use a lower bit rate, you should always use dither and that Power-4-#1 will usually be the best choice. Many CD-burning programs include dithering as an option, but with fewer choices. Here, we started at 24-bit and are bouncing to 24-bit, so we don't need it, but if you know for sure that you are going to burn it onto a CD, you might want to do a second bounce at 16-bit with dithering.

MP3S AND M4AS

MP3s are a ubiquitous compressed audio file format. Their chief virtue is that they are small in size and therefore easy to share on social media and through email, and are good if you do a lot of listening on your phone, which has limited storage. A Google search will tell you that it is possible to have high-quality MP3s.

At the risk of again being the cranky old pro, I am going to tell you that they do not sound very good, even at their highest quality. The compression creates sizzle and distortion, and a lot of the subtle sonic information gets lost.

That said, yes, they have their purpose, and I know you are going to use them. You can create them instead of PCM files or in addition to them. If both are checked, Logic will first bounce the **PCM** and then immediately bounce an **MP3**.

I recommend that you check **Use Variable Bit Rate Encoding (VBR)** with **Quality** set to **Highest**, and check **Use best encoding** and **Filter frequencies below 10 Hz**.

Checking **Add to Music** will add it to the Apple Music app's library, formerly iTunes:

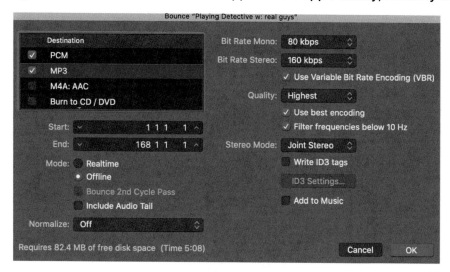

Figure 16.7 – MP3 settings

M4A, also known as Apple Lossless, is another compressed format, developed by Apple. It definitely sounds considerably better than MP3 but is not even close to being used as universally, so for now, we will pass on further discussion of it.

REALTIME VERSUS OFFLINE

Realtime means just that, the bounce happens in real time and you hear it. Offline happens faster, although with third-party DSP plugins, such as those from Universal Audio, it can bounce more slowly, and you don't hear it.

They both have their advantages. If I have recorded a 45-minute voiceover for someone, I sure as heck don't want to sit there for 45 minutes and listen while it bounces. Also, if my computer is struggling with CPU issues, it sometimes will get you past the system overload messages.

Most of the time, however, I do want to do a real-time bounce, because when I sit back in my chair and just listen, I sometimes notice things I did not notice while I was mixing.

You cannot make adjustments while a mix is bouncing. Pressing **Command + period** stops the process so that you can make the adjustments you wish to make and then resume bouncing.

We also see the options of **Bounce 2nd Cycle Pass** and **Include Audio Tail**.

Apple says "in certain situations, you may want to hear a region's FX tail at the start of the bounce. In a one cycle pass, the FX tail will not be recorded because the bounce will have already finished. By recording the final bounce at the start of the second pass, the first pass' FX tail will also be included." Personally, I never use it.

Include Audio Tail is an option to include processing, such as delays and reverb, which takes place after the song ends. I don't use it because some plugins cause the bounce to be much longer than necessary. If I hear the audio tail being prematurely cut off, I think extending the length of the Cycle a bar or two longer is a better solution.

We discussed **Normalize** in *Chapter 12, Getting the Arrangement Right*. Friends don't let friends normalize. Don't do it.

EXPORTING TRACKS TO SEND TO A MIX ENGINEER

If you have a project where you feel you cannot do the mix justice and have the resources to hire an engineer, they may not work in Logic Pro X or may not have the same software instruments and sample libraries that you do, so you will need to export the tracks to send to them. The process was fully explained in *Chapter 12, Getting the Arrangement Right*, so I will not reiterate it here.

MASTERING YOUR MIX

Mastering is the final step in preparing recordings for commercial release. Mastering engineers typically do the following:

- Eliminate pops and clicks and other noise flaws.
- Adjust the volumes between songs for consistency so that listeners do not have to keep turning the volume up and down when listening to an album.
- Adjust the volume so that the loudness conforms to the standards of the intended playback medium (streaming services, CDs, and so on).
- Adjust the EQ and width of the songs, and apply compression or expansion.
- Arrange the songs' order and add fade outs, where required.
- Insert ISRC codes and CD text.

THE CHANGED ROLE OF THE MASTERING ENGINEER

Mastering engineers were considered an elite class of engineers. They had very specific knowledge of how the grooves on vinyl records worked and often thousands of dollars of analog gear to master with, which they knew really well. They were considered essential by record labels and artists, and the famous ones, such as Bernie Grundman, Doug Sax, and Bob Katz, were paid a lot of money for their expertise.

While vinyl is now coming back to a degree, for most recordings, how it works on vinyl is no longer a priority. Because when we hear music louder, we think it sounds better, today's mastering engineers are having to deal, mostly, with trying to make the music as loud as possible, often to the point of almost eliminating dynamic range. Those who have been doing this a long while are not thrilled, but they have to answer to their clients, so they do.

Also, in this era, they may be using mostly, or even exclusively, high-quality digital plugins to master, rather than analog gear.

Of course, they still do the other things mentioned earlier as well. It was a source of pride for me, as you know that I don't consider myself a "real" engineer, that when I gave a mastering engineer the tracks for my album *Honestly*, he said that he really didn't have to do very much because I had done a good job of level matching and mixing. That said, his finished versions did sound noticeably better to me.

If you are your own engineer sending mixes to a mastering engineer, generally you want not to add much processing to the stereo output and leave the mixes peaking at -6 dB, so that they have some headroom to work with, especially if they are using analog gear. But they are pros and will deal with what you give them.

CAN YOU MASTER YOUR OWN TRACKS IN LOGIC PRO X?

In theory, sure. Logic Pro X comes with some very good plugins for this purpose. That said, we all probably have heard the statement that an attorney who is representing himself has a fool for a client.

This applies here. You do not know and won't for a long time, if ever, all that a mastering engineer knows. There are some very good and affordable mastering engineers, so if you are aiming for a commercial release, you need to budget for one. If you are going to only distribute on the internet, though, and you want it to sound as good as it can but cannot afford a mastering engineer, you can do what I prefer to think of as pre-mastering in Logic Pro.

The easiest way to begin to learn how is to use the collections of plugins that you find in the **Channel Strip** settings for the stereo output. Hold the mouse down at the very top of the **Stereo Output** channel strip and scroll down to the **Factory** presets intended for mastering:

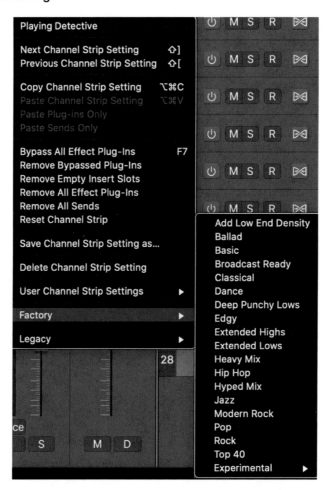

Figure 16.8 – Factory mastering presets

If you load **Broadcast Ready**, you see that it adds a Compressor, a Linear Phase EQ, a Multipressor (multiband compressor), a bypassed Exciter, and finally, an Adaptive Limiter:

Figure 16.9 – The Broadcast Ready mastering preset

If you play back your project and bypass each plugin and then make them active as you are playing back, you will learn a lot. You can, of course, change the settings and hear how the sound changes.

Switch to **Hip Hop** and you will see a different combination of plugins with different settings, and you will hear quite a change in the sound:

Figure 16.10 – The Hip Hop mastering preset

Descriptions of all these plugins can be found in the built-in Logic **Help** menu:

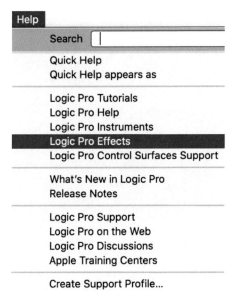

Figure 16.11 – The Logic Pro Effects help

We are done!

SUMMARY

In this chapter, we covered all the file formats available for bouncing, as well as other options. We mentioned the information for exporting tracks, which was discussed in *Chapter 12, Getting the Arrangement Right,* and ended with a discussion of mastering and what I like to refer to as pre-mastering.

I hope you will find this book helpful as you begin your relationship with Logic Pro X. As with all good relationships, it requires a substantial investment in time and real commitment, but the rewards are really great!

Logic Pro X is incredibly deep, and new features are being constantly added, so it grows even deeper. I have been using Logic since 1.0 in 1993, and I am still constantly learning more about it in my daily work.

Good luck, and have fun with Logic Pro X.

INDEX

A

Advanced Quantize parameters
  used, for quantizing regions 94
All view, Mixer views
  Environment 210, 211
Apple Loops
  about 44, 47
  loading, to Quick Sampler 152-156
Apple Lossless 287
Arpeggiator MIDI FX plugin 99, 100
arrangement
  about 183
  section, adding to 186
Arrangement Global Track 127, 128
Audio
  versus MIDI 24
Audio File Editor 85
audio files, timing
  fixing, with Flex Time 177, 178
audio interface 24, 25
Audio Preferences 56, 57
Audio Track Editor
  about 84, 85
  imported audio file, working with 83, 84
automation
  copying 276

copying, between tracks 277
copying, within track 276
deleting 279
history 263-265
MIDI controllers, customizing
    for 279, 280
Remix FX, capturing with 172, 173
automation, trimming
  about 274
  Offline Trim 275
  Real-time Trim 275, 276
Auto Sampler 158, 160

B

balance
  versus panning 228-231
Bounce window
  opening 282-284
Bounce window, Destination menu
  M4As 286, 287
  MP3s 286, 287
  PCM file formats 285, 286
Bounce window, Mode menu
  realtime mode, versus offline
    mode 287, 288

C

cells
  editing, with Live Loops grid 165, 166
  recording into, with Live Loos grid 168
  scenes, creating from 166, 167
  understanding, with Starter grid 161-164
Channel EQ 239, 240
Chillwave 47
ChromaVerb 251
continuous controllers (CCs)
  about 92
  MIDI, recording with 98
crescendo
  creating, by MIDI velocity 119
customized Screensets
  creating 211
  duplicating, to create another 214, 215
  locked custom Screenset,
    creating 211-213
Cycle
  creating, from Marker 219
Cycle and Create Track Alternatives
  MIDI, recording with 97, 98
Cycle and Create Tracks
  MIDI, recording with 96
Cycle and Merge
  MIDI, recording with 96
Cycle and Take Folders
  MIDI, recording with 98
Cycle audio recording options 67
Cycle recording
  about 63
  options 66
  Project Alternatives 66
  Quick Swipe Comping 65
  Region Gain 66
  with Take Folders 63-65

D

Delay Designer 246
Delay plugins
  about 234, 246-250
  Echo delay 248
  Sample delay 248
  Stereo Delay 249
  Tape delay 249
Digital Riff Guitar 47
Display Preferences 59
Drum Kit Designer drum kit
  customizing 130
Drum Machine Designer 133, 134
Drum Machine Designer editor 135
Drum Machine Designer track
  creating, by exporting drum slices 158
Drummer 123-127
Drummer Loops 136, 138
Drummer region
  converting, into MIDI region 129
Drum Synth 136
Dynamics processor plugins
  about 232
  Compressors 242, 243
  Limiters 243
  Noise Gates 244, 245

E

Equalizers (EQ)
  about 232
  used, for solving problems 238

F

Files Browser 43

Flex Pitch
pitch of vocal, fixing with 178-181
Flex Time
audio files timing, fixing with 177, 178
Folder Stacks
about 204
and Mixer 207
creating 204-206
FX plugins
dynamics, controlling 241
managing 235-237
working with 232
FX plugins, categories
about 232
Delay plugins 234, 246
Dynamics processor plugins 232
Equalizers (EQ) plugins 232
Modulation plugins 233, 245
Reverb plugins 234, 235, 250

G

Giant Beats 220
Giant Time display 220
Graphical User Interface (GUI) 89
Groove Tracks 104

H

hard quantizing 94
high pass 239

I

imported audio file
working with, in Audio Track
Editor 83, 84
Impulse Responses (IRs) 251

inputs and outputs (I/O) 25
Inspector Area 33
instruments
loading, into Sampler 151

L

Launchkey MIDI controller 170
layered patch
creating, with Summing Stacks 101
Library 123
Live Loops grid
cells, editing with 165, 166
Remix FX 170
scenes, creating from cells with 166, 167
used, for recording into cells 168
Live Loops grid, Starter grid
cells and scenes, understanding
with 161-164
live track automation
about 270
automatic lane creation, with
Latch mode 274
automatic lane creation, with
Touch mode 274
Volume automation, with
Latch mode 272, 273
Volume automation, with
Touch mode 271
live track automation, Automation modes
Latch mode 271
Read mode 270
Touch mode 271
Write mode 271
Logic Pro MIDI editors
MIDI editors, viewing 90, 91
Logic Pro X
Apple Loops 44-47

Command-click tools 49

content 39, 40

key and transposing regions, changing 50

Left-click tool 48

Loop Browser 44-47

opening, for first time 27-29

preferences settings, versus project settings 27

project, saving 47

Snap menu 49, 50

Logic Pro X 10.5, essential hardware

audio interface 24-26

MIDI controller 26

monitor headphones 27

monitor speakers 26

selecting 24

Logic Pro X, Bounce options

about 193

Bounce and Replace All Tracks 197

Bounce Regions In Place 197

Bounce Track In Place 195, 196

Logic Pro X, Browsers

exploring 40

Files Browser 43

Media Browser 42

Project Browser 41

Logic Pro X, default opening behavior

changing 29

Logic Pro X, Export options

Export Tracks and Regions 198, 200

Logic Pro X Library

about 34, 35

Control bar, customizing 36-39

Toolbar 36

Toolbar, customizing 36-39

Logic Pro X menus 31

Logic Pro X's built-in help 88

Logic Pro X's Software Instruments

about 87

GarageBand, versus Logic Pro instruments 88, 90

Logic Pro X terminology

about 31

tracks, versus Channel Strips 33, 34

Logic Pro X, Track Header Components

Freeze tracks, adding 201, 202

Logic Pro X windows

about 31

Main Window 31-33

Logic Remote 169

Loop Browser 44, 47

Low-Frequency Oscillation (LFO) 245

low pass 239

M

Marker key commands

project, navigating with 217

Markers

creating 215

creating, in Marker track 215-217

Cycle, creating from 219

editing, in Marker List 219, 220

Marquee tool

regions parts, copying with 79, 80

mastering engineer

changed role 289

Media Browser 42

Merge

MIDI, recording with 92

microphones, types

condenser mics 25

dynamic mics 25

ribbon mics 26

MIDI continuous controllers 92
MIDI controllers
  about 26
  customizing, for automation 279, 280
MIDI region
  Drummer region, converting into 129
  viewing, in Logic Pro MIDI editors 90, 91
mix engineer
  tracks, exporting for sending to 288
Mixer
  and Folder Stacks 207
Mixer views
  about 208
  All view 209
  Single view 209
  Tracks view 208
Modulation plugins 233, 245
monitor headphones 27
monitor speakers 26
Musical instrument Digital
      Interface (MIDI)
  about 24
  converting, to audio files 192, 193
  recording, techniques 95
  recording, with CCs 98
  recording, with Cycle and Create
      Track Alternatives 97, 98
  recording, with Cycle and
      Create Tracks 96
  recording, with Cycle and Cycle
      and Take Folders 98
  recording, with Cycle and Merge 96
  recording, with flawed timing 93
  recording, with Merge 92
  recording, with Replace mode 95, 96
  versus Audio 24
mute/solo buttons
    on channel strip, in Mixer 74
    on Track Header 72, 73

N

Novation Launchpad controller 170

O

offline region automation
  about 266
  plug-in bypass automation,
      in region 269, 270
  region panning automation 266-269

P

panning
  about 226-228
  used, for achieving mix goals 226, 228
  versus balance 228-231
patches
  about 34
  creating 101
Pattern Browser 145-147
Pattern Loops 147
Pattern Regions
  about 141, 143
  Steps, creating 143
percussionist
  adding 132, 133
Piano Roll Editor
  crescendo, creating by MDI velocity 119
  MIDI controller, steps entering 118
  step entering 107
  vibrato, creating with
      modulation 119, 120
Playhead 33

plug-in bypass automation
  in region 269, 270
Pre Fader Metering 258, 259
Preferences
  Audio Preferences 56, 57
  Display Preferences 59
  Recording Preferences 58, 59
  setting 56
Producer Kit 131, 132
Project Alternative
  creating 184-186
Project Browser 41
project mix
  consideration 259, 260
  example 257-259
  goals 223, 224
  goals, achieving with panning 226-228
  goals, achieving with volume 225
Project Settings
  about 60
  levels, setting 60-63
Project Templates 54-56
project tempo
  adjusting, with imported audio
    using Smart Tempo 175, 176

Q

quantizing 94
Quick Sampler
  Apple Loops, loading to 152-156
  audio files, importing 157
  drum slices, exporting to create Drum
    Machine Designer track 158
  recording into 157, 158
  working with 151, 152
Quick Swipe Comping 65

R

recording
  with Cycle 63
  without Cycle 67, 68
Recording Preferences 58, 59
recording without click
  with Smart Tempo 69
Redmatica 158
Region Inspector 33
region panning automation 266-269
regions
  consolidating 192, 193
  copying 78
  copying, by holding Option + dragging 78
  editing, with Shuffle Mode 80, 81
  looping 82
  quantizing 94
  quantizing, by setting default
    quantization settings 95
  quantizing, with Advanced
    Quantize parameters 94
  repeating 78, 81
  zooming in 77
  zooming out 77
region solo button
  in Control Bar 74, 75
regions, parts
  copying, with Marquee tool 79, 80
Remix FX
  about 170
  capturing, with Automation 172, 173
  overview 170-172
Replace mode
  MIDI, recording with 95, 96
reverb
  about 250
  ChromaVerb 251

SilverVerb 251

Space Designer 253

vocal project 254-256

Reverb plugins

about 234, 250

algorithmic 251

convolution 251

rubber-banding 47

S

Sampler

instruments, loading 151

scenes

understanding, with Starter grid 161-164

section, adding to arrangement

about 186

Insert Silence at Locators 186, 189, 190

Repeat Section Between
Locators 190, 191

section, deleting from arrangement

about 191

Cut Section Between Locators 192

Shuffle Mode

regions, editing with 80, 81

SilverVerb 251

Smart Tempo

recording, without click 69

used, for adjusting project tempo with
imported audio file 175, 176

Space Designer 252, 253

split layered patch

creating, with Summing Stacks 102, 103

Step Editor 121

step entering 107

step entering, in Piano Roll Editor

about 107-110

Scale Quantize 112, 113

Time Quantize 113, 114

Velocity slider 110, 111

Velocity Tool 111

Step Input Keyboard

MIDI Transform 116, 117

Time Handles 118

using 114, 115

Step Sequencer

Pattern Regions, using with 141, 143

rows and sounds, editing 144

working with 139, 140

Step Sequencer Local Inspector 144

stereo mix

bouncing 281, 282

mastering 288-291

Summing Stacks

layered patch, creating with 101

split layered patch, creating
with 102, 103

T

Take Folders 63-65

Tape recorder style punching in/out 68

template

saving 70

track automation Event List 277, 279

Track Inspector 33

tracks

exporting, for sending to
mix engineer 288

tracks and regions

colorizing 75, 76

muting 71

renaming 75, 76

soloing 71

Tracks area
  about 33
  performance, recording to 168, 169

U

Ultrabeat 133

V

Varispeed 181, 182
vibrato
  creating, with modulation 119, 120
vocal, pitch
  fixing, with Flex Pitch 178-181

OTHER BOOKS YOU MAY ENJOY

If you enjoyed this book, you may be interested in these other books by Packt:

HANDS-ON MUSIC GENERATION WITH MAGENTA

Alexandre DuBreuil

ISBN: 978-1-83882-441-9

- Use RNN models in Magenta to generate MIDI percussion, and monophonic and polyphonic sequences
- Use WaveNet and GAN models to generate instrument notes in the form of raw audio
- Employ Variational Autoencoder models like MusicVAE and GrooVAE to sample, interpolate, and humanize existing sequences
- Prepare and create your dataset on specific styles and instruments
- Train your network on your personal datasets and fix problems when training networks
- Apply MIDI to synchronize Magenta with existing music production tools like DAWs

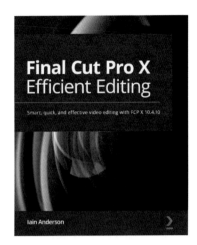

FINAL CUT PRO X EFFICIENT EDITING

Iain Anderson

ISBN: 978-1-83921-324-3

- Understand the media import process and delve into media management
- Effectively organize your footage so you can find the right shot quickly
- Discover how to assemble a rough cut edit
- Explore trimming and advanced editing techniques to finesse and finalize the edit
- Enhance the edit with color correction, effects, transitions, titles, captions, and much more
- Sweeten the audio by controlling volume, using compression, and adding effects
- Share the final edited video and archive the job

LEAVE A REVIEW - LET OTHER READERS KNOW WHAT YOU THINK

Please share your thoughts on this book with others by leaving a review on the site that you bought it from. If you purchased the book from Amazon, please leave us an honest review on this book's Amazon page. This is vital so that other potential readers can see and use your unbiased opinion to make purchasing decisions, we can understand what our customers think about our products, and our authors can see your feedback on the title that they have worked with Packt to create. It will only take a few minutes of your time, but is valuable to other potential customers, our authors, and Packt. Thank you!

PACKT IS SEARCHING FOR AUTHORS LIKE YOU

If you're interested in becoming an author for Packt, please visit authors.packtpub.com and apply today. We have worked with thousands of developers and tech professionals, just like you, to help them share their insight with the global tech community. You can make a general application, apply for a specific hot topic that we are recruiting an author for, or submit your own idea.

Made in the USA
Monee, IL
13 November 2020